Imagine
The Fully Devoted Life
for students

IMAGINE THE FULLY DEVOTED LIFE
FOR STUDENTS

Published by Outcome Publishing
www.imaginethedevotedlife.com

This book or parts thereof may not be reproduced in any form, stored in a retrieval system, or transmitted in any form by any means – electronic, mechanical, photocopy, recording, or otherwise – without prior written permission of the publisher, except as provided by United States of America copyright law.

Unless otherwise indicated, Bible quotations are taken from The Holy Bible, New International Version. Copyright © 1973, 1978, 1984, by International Bible Society.

Scripture quotations marked KJV are from the Holy Bible, King James Version, copyright © 1987, Holman Bible Publishers. All rights reserved.

Copyright © Outcome Publishing
All rights reserved

First Edition

Printed in the United States of America

1. Religion: Spirituality General
2. Self-Help: Spiritual
3. Religion: Christian Life – Personal Growth

We are so excited that you are joining us on a journey toward understanding and living the Christian life. God created us not only to know Him but to make a positive difference in our world. You'll learn about God's gift given to us in Jesus during this study. You'll also learn how we can bring change as we become fully devoted followers of Christ. We have a story to tell. God has given us a new life to live for an important purpose. We are to be love to a lost world. Our hope is that this study will help you grow in areas of weakness and thrive in areas of strength. Just imagine what God can do through you!

The Imagine Leadership Team

Table of Contents

Introduction   9

Section One Test – **A Life to Measure…11**
  Chapter One   The Assessment: Imagine a life that knows where it stands…13

Section Two   **Testimony – A Story to Tell…29**
  Chapter Two   The Story: Imagine a life that remembers where it started…31
  Chapter Three   The Purpose: Imagine a life that shares God openly…45

Section Three   **Time – A Schedule to Keep…65**
  Chapter Four   The Craving: Imagine a life that hungers for God…67
  Chapter Five   The Disciplines: Imagine a life that manages its opportunities…79

Section Four   **Talents – The Gifts to Use…103**
  Chapter Six   The Passion: Imagine a life that exercises concern for others…105
  Chapter Seven   The Work: Imagine a life that engages the community…119

Section Five   **Treasures – The Resources to Share…143**
  Chapter Eight   The Giver: Imagine a life that invests in eternity…145
  Chapter Nine   The Margin: Imagine a life that conserves available resources.157

Section Six   **Totally – A Life to Surrender…167**
  Chapter Ten   The Commitments: Imagine a life that
                      dedicates all to God…169

End Notes   **183**

Appendix A   **Quiet Time Guides…185**

Appendix B   **The Spider Graph…225**

And to know this love that surpasses knowledge — that you may be filled to the measure of all the fullness of God. Now to him who is able to do immeasurably more than all we ask or imagine, according to his power that is at work within us, to him be glory in the church and in Christ Jesus throughout all generations, for ever and ever! Amen.
Ephesians 3:19-21

Introduction

Wouldn't it be amazing to master every area of the Christian life? Often we hear about stewardship and relate it to our giving of financial resources as we invest in the kingdom of God. This is an important part of our stewardship life. However, it's not the only part.

You are about to take a journey through something called "Total Life Stewardship." What does that mean, you ask? Great question! The word stewardship means *the responsibility of watching over and protecting something that is consider to be of worth*. We should feel this way not only about financial resources, but about the Christian life as a whole.

We should want to watch over the areas of the Christian life that help us make a difference in the world. These areas consist of sharing our TESTIMONY, managing our TIME as we grow personally into stronger disciples, using our TALENTS as we serve the people who are in need, and investing TREASURES in a way that impacts the world as we share Good News.

The lessons you'll learn will help you as you develop in all four areas of the spiritual life that lead to greater commitment. Let's look at them in more detail. You'll learn about your:

- **Testimony**: You'll learn how to share the greatest love story of all: your love story, which involves God, His Son, His Spirit, and you! Those who share their story testify about the events that made the difference in leading them toward God.
- **Time**: You'll learn about the disciplines you need to practice to improve Christian living. Practicing these disciplines requires our time. Those who are dedicated to become fully devoted followers of Christ spend time practicing so that they can be prepared to live for Him.

- **Talents**: You'll learn about your unique makeup. God created you with purpose, which means that He gave you certain gifts and talents for a reason. He wants you to use them in a way that encourages others to see Him and know Him.
- **Treasures**: Although treasures are under your care, they belong to God. You'll learn that God has placed resources under your care to be used to bring glory to Him. You use those resources as investment tools. Those who invest their resources make an eternal impact.

Imagine what would happen through you if you shared your testimony, gave God the time He deserves, used your talents and gifts to serve Him by serving others, and invested God's treasures in a way that changed the world. You really would make a difference for Him. Do you want to make a difference? Doing so requires maturity. The theme Scripture for this book appears below. Read it out loud!

> To prepare God's people for works of service, so that the body of Christ may be built up until we all reach unity in the faith and in the knowledge of the Son of God and become mature, attaining to the whole measure of the fullness of Christ.
>
> Ephesians 4:12-13

God wants us to attain the whole measure of the fullness of Christ. Do you want to be fully devoted to Him? Open your heart and mind, and listen to what God wants to say to you as you learn how.

Section One
The Test:
A Life to Measure

Chapter One
The Assessment:
Imagine a life that knows where it stands.

> Don't let anyone look down on you because you are young, but set an example for the believers in speech, in life, in love, in faith and in purity.
> 1 Timothy 4:12

We'll be going through a process together to accomplish something really important called spiritual transformation. As works in progress, we need to transform continually to be more like Christ. God has a goal for us: it's Christlikeness. The vision we have for our lives should be to achieve this resemblance to Jesus. Our accomplishing the goal we set before us brings success.

The movie *Transformers* is a good example of our spiritual transformation. In the movie, aliens take on the appearance of mechanical things like automobiles and trucks. The special effects of the movie are amazing. Seeing a car turn into a robot whose mission is to protect and save the world is so cool. The robots look one way, but they become something very different for a purpose. The same is true of us spiritually. We continually change to become someone who looks like Christ, someone who lives to protect and save the world.

We're all being spiritually transformed. Although good robots were in the movie, evil ones were, too. They had to be, right? Otherwise, the movie would be pretty dull. Some peoples' transformation doesn't cause them to look more like

Jesus; instead, they begin to look more like the world. They transform, not to protect and save the world, but to protect and save themselves. Those who find themselves in this condition live very frustrated lives. What they think will bring them happiness actually steals the joy God wants them to have. We need the right type of transformation. So how do we transform? That's a great question.

Spiritual transformation begins with knowing who we are now and knowing what God wants us to be. We've already read out loud the theme Scripture for this study. God instructs us to become mature and attain the fullness of Christ, the One who had compassion for humanity and showed His love through His service and sacrifice. This description should also characterize us. Does it describe who you are? Are you telling your story about how you came to know Him? Are you growing to be more like Him? Are you meeting needs in order to reveal who He is? Are you using resources to help provide ministries that impact our community and world in a positive way?

A great beginning point is getting a picture of who we are. We'll do so in four primary areas of the Christian life. We learned what they were in the introduction. We will concentrate on our testimony, time, talents, and treasures. Once we know who we are in these areas, we can know who we need to become.

On the next few pages you'll find a Spiritual Assessment Test that will help you get a picture of your spiritual condition. You'll answer questions about who you are and then chart your answers on a graph that will give you a quick look at yourself as it relates to your spirituality.

Instructions: Using of scale of one to ten, with one meaning never true and ten meaning always true, answer the following questions.

TESTIMONY

Sharing my story with those who don't know God

1. I have a burden for those who do not know Christ.

"When he saw the crowds, he had compassion on them, because they were harassed and helpless, like sheep without a shepherd" (Matthew 9:36).

Score: _____

2. I identify those in my circle of influence who are lost.

"For the Son of Man came to seek and to save what was lost" (Luke 19:10).

Score: _____

3. I pray regularly for those in my circle of influence who are lost.

"My prayer is not for them alone. I pray also for those who will believe in me through their message" (John 17:20).

Score: _____

4. I share my faith with others regularly.

"For we cannot help speaking about what we have seen and heard" (Acts 4:20).

Score: _____

5. I use my spiritual gifts to serve others in an effort to build relationships with the lost.

"It was he who gave some to be apostles, some to be prophets, some to be evangelists, and some to be pastors and teachers, to prepare God's people for works of service" (Ephesians 4:11-12).

Score: _____

6. I invite those in my circle of influence to experiences where they will be exposed to the message of Christ.

"Go to the street corners and invite to the banquet anyone you find" (Matthew 22:9).

Score: _____

7. allow God to use me as a witness by living a life free of sin.

"Finally, brothers, whatever is true, whatever is noble, whatever is right, whatever is pure, whatever is lovely, whatever is admirable—if anything is excellent or praiseworthy—think about such things" (Philippians 4:8).
Score: _____

8. My words and my actions support one another.

"'About Jesus of Nazareth,' they replied. 'He was a prophet, powerful in word and deed before God and all the people'" (Luke 24:19).
Score: _____

9. I live a life of joy.

"But the fruit of the Spirit is...joy" (Galatians 5:22).
Score: _____

10. I am willing to put myself at risk in an effort to share the good news of Christ with those who are lost.

"For even the Son of Man did not come to be served, but to serve, and to give his life as a ransom for many" (Mark 10:45).
Score: _____

TIME

Growing in my relationship with God

1. I have a close companionship with God.

"A man of many companions may come to ruin, but there is a friend who sticks closer than a brother" (Proverbs 18:24).

Score: _____

2. I spend time alone with God on a regular basis.

"In the morning, O LORD, you hear my voice; in the morning I lay my requests before you and wait in expectation" (Psalm 5:3).

Score: _____

3. I regularly practice the discipline of prayer.

"And pray in the Spirit on all occasions with all kinds of prayers and requests. With this in mind, be alert and always keep on praying for all the saints" (Ephesians 6:18).

Score: _____

4. I regularly practice the discipline of Bible study.

"Your word is a lamp to my feet and a light for my path" (Psalm 119:105).

Score: _____

5. I regularly memorize God's Word.

"I have hidden your word in my heart that I might not sin against you" (Psalm 119:11).

Score: _____

6. I live a life of self control.

"But the fruit of the Spirit is...self control" (Galatians 5:22-23).

Score: _____

7. I regularly spend time with a group of believers who hold me accountable to living obediently.

"Every day they continued to meet together in the temple courts. They broke bread in their homes and ate together with glad and sincere hearts" (Acts 2:46).

Score: _____

8. I worship God corporately weekly.

"You Samaritans worship what you do not know; we worship what we do know, for salvation is from the Jews" (John 4:22).

Score: _____

9. I am regularly mentored by another believer.

"Don't let anyone look down on you because you are young, but set an example for the believers in speech, in life, in love, in faith and in purity" (1 Timothy 4:12).

Score: _____

10. I work with God to overcome my weaknesses.

"If you are pleased with me, teach me your ways so I may know you and continue to find favor with you" (Exodus 33:13).

Score: _____

TALENTS

Using my gifts and talents in service

1. I regularly put the needs of others before my own needs.
"The Son of Man did not come to be served, but to serve, and to give his life as a ransom for many" (Matthew 20:28).
Score: _____

2. I am concerned about those who are in need.
"But a Samaritan, as he traveled, came where the man was; and when he saw him, he took pity on him" (Luke 10:33).
Score: _____

3. I pray for those who are in need.
"We always thank God, the Father of our Lord Jesus Christ, when we pray for you" (Colossians 1:3).
Score: _____

4. I actively seek ways to help those who are in need.
"For I was hungry and you gave me something to eat, I was thirsty and you gave me something to drink, I was a stranger and you invited me in, I needed clothes and you clothed me, I was sick and you looked after me, I was in prison and you came to visit me" (Matthew 25:35-36).
Score: _____

5. I am kind to strangers.
"I was a stranger and you invited me in" (Matthew 25:35).
Score: _____

6. I know what my spiritual gifts are.

"Therefore you do not lack any spiritual gift as you eagerly wait for our Lord Jesus Christ to be revealed" (1 Corinthians 1:7).

Score: _____

7. I have an active ministry.

"The King will reply, 'I tell you the truth, whatever you did for one of the least of these brothers of mine, you did for me'" (Matthew 25:40).

Score: _____

8. I serve others even when it is not convenient.

"You, my brothers, were called to be free. But do not use your freedom to indulge the sinful nature; rather, serve one another in love" (Galatians 5:13).

Score: _____

9. I pray for those who are in leadership within the church.

"Pray for us. We are sure that we have a clear conscience and desire to live honorably in every way" (Hebrews 13:18).

Score: _____

10. I make time sacrifices to meet the needs of others.

"Be imitators of God, therefore, as dearly loved children and live a life of love, just as Christ loved us and gave himself up for us as a fragrant offering and sacrifice to God" (Ephesians 5:1-2).

Score: _____

TREASURES
Managing resources to make a difference

1. I give my tithe to assist in God's kingdom work.
"'Bring the whole tithe into the storehouse, that there may be food in my house. Test me in this,' says the LORD Almighty, 'and see if I will not throw open the floodgates of heaven and pour out so much blessing that you will not have room enough for it'" (Malachi 3:10).
Score: _____

2. I trust God in every situation.
"Do not let your hearts be troubled. Trust in God; trust also in me" (John 14:1).
Score: _____

3. I regularly make sacrifices to please God.
"Greater love has no one than this, that he lay down his life for his friends" (John 15:13).
Score: _____

4. I give cheerfully to advance God's kingdom.
"Each man should give what he has decided in his heart to give, not reluctantly or under compulsion, for God loves a cheerful giver" (2 Corinthians 9:7).
Score: _____

5. I have a desire to be obedient in giving (to give what is in my heart).
"But just as you excel in everything—in faith, in speech, in knowledge, in complete earnestness and in your love for us— see that you also excel in this grace of giving"
(2 Corinthians 8:7).
Score: _____

6. My actions reveal that I believe money and resources are God's possessions which are under my care.
"All the believers were one in heart and mind. No one claimed that any of his possessions was his own, but they shared everything they had" (Acts 4:32).
Score: _____

7. I consider how my purchases affect my ability to give to God's kingdom before I make them.
"Then he said to them, 'Watch out! Be on your guard against all kinds of greed; a man's life does not consist in the abundance of his possessions'" (Luke 12:15).
Score: _____

8. I ask, "Will this purchase honor God?" before spending money.
"Jesus answered, 'If you want to be perfect, go, sell your possessions and give to the poor, and you will have treasure in heaven. Then come, follow me'" (Matthew 19:21).
Score: _____

9. I manage my resources to ensure margin (available funds) to help those in need.
"But Zacchaeus stood up and said to the Lord, 'Look, Lord! Here and now I give half of my possessions to the poor, and if I have cheated anybody out of anything, I will pay back four times the amount'" (Luke 19:8).
Score: _____

10. I am willing to sacrifice to invest in the success of others.
"Selling their possessions and goods, they gave to anyone as he had need" (Acts 2:45).
Score: _____

Plotting My Score

Look at the graph on the next page. You'll notice four quadrants. Each represents the four focus areas of the Spiritual Assessment Test, beginning with **Testimony** in the top right section. Circles appear from the inside to the outside. They represent the one to ten measurement for each question, with the circle closest to the center being one and the farthest circle being ten. There are ten lines within each quadrant. Each numbered line corresponds to the question number on the assessment. If you answered the first question under the focus area of **Testimony** with the number seven, you would make a dot where the seventh circle from the center intersects the line numbered one in the **Testimony** quadrant. After plotting the answers, connect the dots. The graph begins to look like a spider's web. Look at a sample Spider Graph on the following page.

Sample Spider Graph

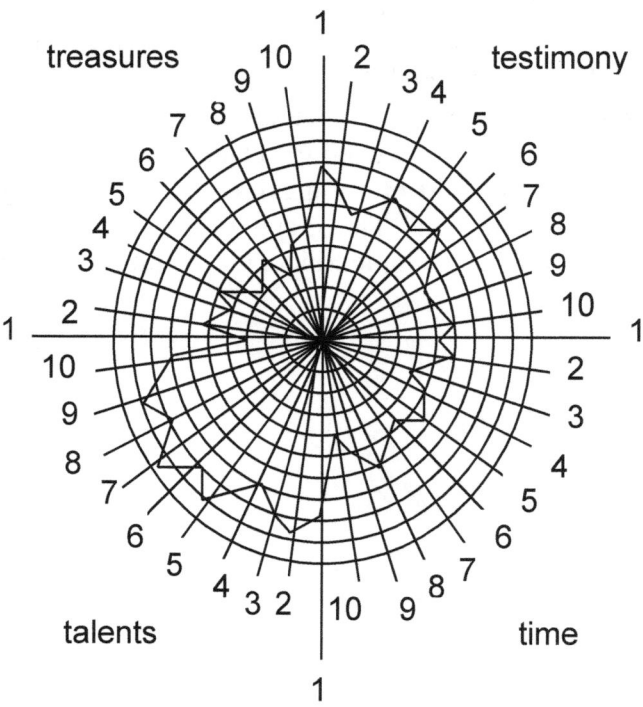

What do we learn from the graph above? This person loves to use his talents to serve others. We see this result in the **Talents** quadrant. Although he serves, he isn't as faithful in sharing his story of what Christ has done for him with non-believers. We see this trait in the **Testimony** quadrant. We notice in the **Time** quadrant that he doesn't spend much time with God in order to grow spiritually. Finally, his biggest struggle is in the area of giving. This struggle appears in the **Treasures** quadrant.

Is this cool or what? Isn't it awesome to be able to get a real picture of someone's spiritual condition? It's your turn! On the following page, use the method described above to plot all of your answers and connect the dots.

Make sure you record answers in the correct quadrant. Begin with number **1** at the top and center of the graph and plot your scores for the **testimony** section to the right. Continue to plot your scores for the other areas of the fully devoted life as you move around the graph.

The Spider Graph

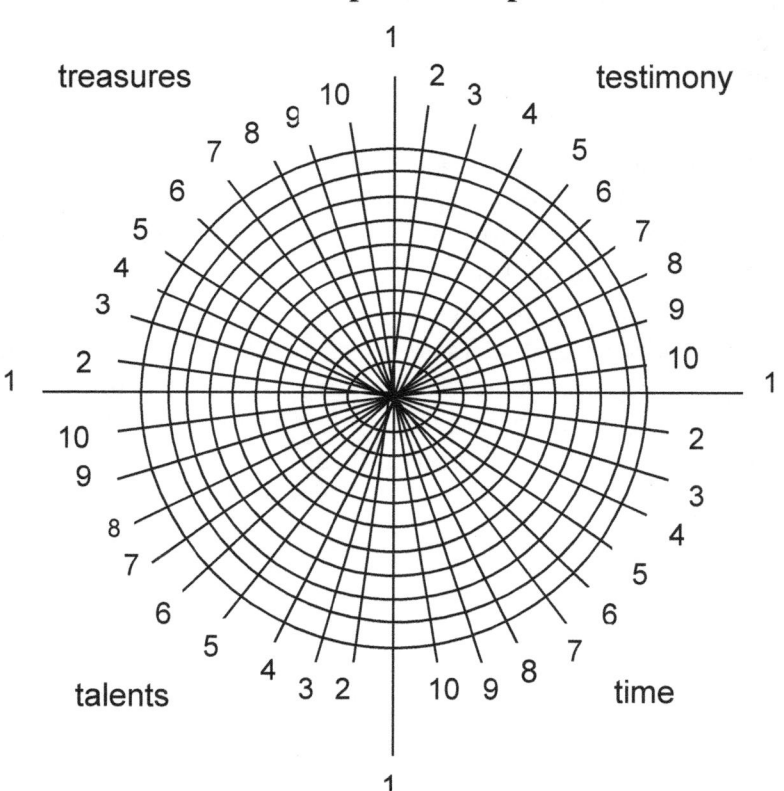

Just for fun, color the area from the center of the chart to the connecting lines. Wouldn't being able to color in the whole circle be great? If we could, we'd see our full devotion. Uncolored areas help us see areas in need of more commitment. There is good news for you: we can be stronger. We may never be able to completely color in the entire graph, but we can continue to grow. Now that we have a picture of who we are, let's learn how we can move closer toward living the fully devoted life.

One way to learn is to read this book and take a closer look at who you are. You'll notice questions to answer as you progress in your reading. You'll see the letter *Q* (which stands for question) followed by a question. Answer them! Don't answer quickly. Put some thought into your responses. The more thought you put into this study, the more effect it will have on your spiritual transformation. Something else can also help you grow.

Each question in the Spiritual Assessment Test had Scripture associated with it. These passages help us understand God's expectation as it relates to these issues. Learning what God has to say to us is important for us. To help you learn, Make the commitment to spend time with God five days a week for the next eight weeks. Find a time of the day that you can commit to be consistent in your time alone with God. You'll find QT (Quiet Time) guides in Appendix A in the back of the book with Scriptures and reflection questions for forty days. Every week and day are numbered. For example, you will see the heading: Week One, Day One. Each day, you are to read the questions, and then ask God to help you grow as you apply His Word to your life. Let's begin right now! Turn to the back of the book, and complete the Quiet Time for Week One, Day One.

God, thank You for revealing to me my spiritual condition. I ask You to teach me and mold me into who You want me to be.

Section Two
Testimony:
A Story to Tell

Chapter Two
The Story:
Imagine a life that remembers where it started.

> Now get up and stand on your feet. I have appeared to you to appoint you as a servant and as a witness of what you have seen of me and what I will show you.
> Acts 26:16

Most people love vacations. One of the most relaxing for many is the beach where we feel the sand on our feet, look over the ocean and watch the boats go by and smell the salt air. What was your favorite vacation? Where did you go? What did you do? Why was it so awesome? Would you do it again?

You just told a story about something that happened in your life. Stories take on a new life when they're ours. They mean something to us because they happened to us. You may have a vacation story, but if you're a believer, you also have a story about what God has done for you. Traveling down the road that led to Him is the greatest trip of all. He's the destination we all seek. Can you imagine what would happen if you were open with others about your relationship with God? Can you imagine what would happen in others if you told the story about your spiritual journey? Some of you can say yes because you're active in sharing your testimony, your personal experience, with those around you. Speaking of the love journey we've taken with God is important for us.

Our relationships revolve around stories, which are how we most often communicate. Here are some examples. You come in from your busy day, and someone asks you about what you did during the day. What do you do? You answer by telling them a story. Here's another example. You call your sister, and she tells you about some events that are going on in her life (a story). You get off the phone, and your friend asks what your sister told you. You tell him what you just heard (another story), a description of an experience in your life. You tell about the events. People connect to this. Why? We're interested in personal history. We need to be good storytellers if we're going to impact the lives of those who don't know God.

In one of the most popular verses in the Bible, Jesus speaks of His purpose, the reason that He came into the world. Check it out. "For God so loved the world that he gave his one and only Son, that whoever believes in him shall not perish but have eternal life" (John 3:16).

This verse is part of the story of Jesus. He's the one who spoke these words as He talked about Himself. What was he doing? He was telling the story about the purpose of His life. Jesus came to help people have a relationship with God, and to connect with Jesus, they needed to hear the story of His life.

We become like Him when we share what has happened to us. Are you sharing the message? One of the most difficult disciplines for a believer to practice is witnessing: sharing our story about what God has done for us. Witnessing is difficult because of the fears that many have: fears of rejection and ridicule. We need to keep something in mind. The risk is worth it!

We see a great example of someone who took a risk in sharing about his life. His name is Paul. We read about him in the book of Acts. From his story, we learn so much about sharing our faith with those who need to be rescued spiritually. Take a look at the Scripture.

> Then Agrippa said to Paul, "You have permission to speak for yourself." So Paul motioned with his hand and began his defense: "King Agrippa, I consider myself fortunate to stand before you today as I make my defense against all the accusations of the Jews, and especially so because you are well acquainted with all the Jewish customs and

controversies. Therefore, I beg you to listen to me patiently. The Jews all know the way I have lived ever since I was a child, from the beginning of my life in my own country, and also in Jerusalem. They have known me for a long time and can testify, if they are willing, that according to the strictest sect of our religion, I lived as a Pharisee. And now it is because of my hope in what God has promised our fathers that I am on trial today. This is the promise our twelve tribes are hoping to see fulfilled as they earnestly serve God day and night. O king, it is because of this hope that the Jews are accusing me. Why should any of you consider it incredible that God raises the dead? I too was convinced that I ought to do all that was possible to oppose the name of Jesus of Nazareth. And that is just what I did in Jerusalem. On the authority of the chief priests I put many of the saints in prison, and when they were put to death, I cast my vote against them. Many a time I went from one synagogue to another to have them punished, and I tried to force them to blaspheme. In my obsession against them, I even went to foreign cities to persecute them. On one of these journeys I was going to Damascus with the authority and commission of the chief priests. About noon, O king, as I was on the road, I saw a light from heaven, brighter than the sun, blazing around me and my companions. We all fell to the ground, and I heard a voice saying to me in Aramaic, 'Saul, Saul, why do you persecute me? It is hard for you to kick against the goads.' Then I asked, 'Who are you, Lord?' 'I am Jesus, whom you are persecuting,' the Lord replied. 'Now get up and stand on your feet. I have appeared to you to appoint you as a servant and as a witness of what you have seen of me and what I will show you. I will rescue you from your own people and from the Gentiles. I am sending you to them to open their eyes and turn them from darkness to light, and from the power of Satan to God, so that they may receive forgiveness of sins and a place among those who are sanctified by faith in me.' So then, King Agrippa,

I was not disobedient to the vision from heaven. First to those in Damascus, then to those in Jerusalem and in all Judea, and to the Gentiles also, I preached that they should repent and turn to God and prove their repentance by their deeds.

Acts 26:1-20

If you were on trial, what testimony would you give about your encounter with Christ? We, too, can speak of some things that Paul shared concerning what God has done for us. Let's learn them.

Sharing My Good Fortune

Paul made an important statement. He wrote that he had good fortune. "King Agrippa, I consider myself fortunate to stand before you today as I make my defense against all the accusations of the Jews" (Acts 26:2). Paul was fortunate, and so are we. Get the scene. Paul had been arrested, and he had to defend what he'd done in court. Not too many people would believe they were fortunate to be prisoners and to be on trial, but Paul was. Think about where his fortune began. It didn't begin at having the opportunity to give a defense; it began at his recognizing his need for Christ.

We are fortunate when we recognize our need.

There are many people who are physically ill. One of the most devastating diseases in our society today is cancer. Cancer exists in many different types. Some aggressive types travel quickly through the body, destroying what's in their path. Catching cancer quickly is so important. The earlier it's detected, the more hope of a cure, of healing. There have been many people who have been fortunate in this way. They may say, "I'm so fortunate that we caught it early." What a true statement. Walking around with a disease that you don't know you have is not something to get very excited about, especially if it's a disease that kills. Knowing about the disease is good so that the proper treatment can encourage good health once again.

Just as there are physical diseases, there is also a spiritual disease. All of us walk around with it. The Scriptures call it sin. The word *sin* means "to miss the mark." We pick up on this definition of the word in the book of Romans. Paul wrote: "For all have sinned and fall short of the glory of God" (Romans 3:23).

Sin is like shooting an arrow which falls short of its target. We are supposed to live up to God's glory. In other words, we should live a life that helps others see how great He is. We do this by looking like Christ. He's the target, but we fall short. We miss the mark by disobeying Him. We've all done so. We've all sinned.

Sin is the spiritual cancer of life, and some don't know they have it. They don't know that their sin keeps them away from God, the God of spiritual life. People know that they make mistakes and that mistakes have consequences here on the earth. Think about it. If we become angry and act out in physical violence, we've done something wrong which has an effect, possibly a lasting one. That effect may be lasting, but some don't see it as an everlasting effect. They believe that when this life is over, the consequences for their mistake end. This belief isn't truth.

God created us to be eternal beings. That fact is why we have a longing in our hearts to know God. We hope for there to be more after this life. If you don't believe in this hope, just think about what has happened in our world. Humans have created many gods because of our search for a supreme being who can give us hope, a hope for a future. The problem is that we've created these gods, but we need to serve the God who created us. He's the Creator God who is the God of love.

God loves us, but we have loved ourselves more than we've loved Him. All sin comes from self-centeredness, and this sin separates us from Him. Although we know we do things wrong, many people consider themselves to be moral, to be good. They trust this goodness for their eternal future. They would say something like this: "How could anything bad happen to me if I haven't done anything to harm others?" Being good doesn't connect us with God; it doesn't begin a relationship. Being good is about our ability; knowing God is about having a relationship. Here's the problem. God only invites those with whom He has a relationship into His house. At the end of our lives, only those in the family are invited to the family reunion.

We're all looking for relationships. They give us true meaning in life. If we don't have them, we feel empty. We're created by God for one relationship in particular, a relationship with Him. The question is: how do we become family members? What is the solution?

Two things solve the relationship dilemma. The first solution is knowing about sin. We are fortunate when we know we have spiritual cancer. We know we have a problem. The second solution is doing what's necessary to remove the sin. We need treatment that removes the cancer, a treatment we don't deserve.

We are fortunate when we realize God's mercy.

The removal of sin works this way. We need the One we offended to offer us grace and mercy. The word *grace* means "being given something we don't deserve (forgiveness)." The word *mercy* means "not being given something we do deserve (punishment)." Both grace and mercy come from love. We need a love doctor. The Scripture doesn't call Him this; it calls him the Savior. He rescues us. He's the one who removes what's killing us. He heals us in a unique way: through a blood transfusion.

Blood transfusions given to cancer patients remove the infected blood and replace it with blood that is pure. The doctor removes the disease and replaces it with something that brings healing. Jesus died on the cross and shed His blood to cleanse us of what causes our spiritual sickness. He shed His blood for us to take away our sin. The Scripture teaches us: "But if we walk in the light, as he is in the light, we have fellowship with one another, and the blood of Jesus, his Son, purifies us from all sin" (1 John 1:7). It's great to know all of this, but how does this transaction work? How do we actually receive forgiveness? How does God take away the sin?

We are fortunate that Jesus paid our ransom.

God takes away sin through someone paying the price for our sin. Remember, sin separates us from God. The result of sin is death. We can go back to the beginning of mankind and see this. No disease or death existed in the world when God created humanity. These evils came into existence when we sinned against God. Death has been a reality from that time forward. Physical death is breath being separated from the body, while spiritual death is the spirit being separated from God.

There is good news! The sin we commit can be removed if someone completes the punishment for the sin, like someone being sentenced for a crime, fulfilling the sentence, and being released. Our punishment is the worst of all: death. That's where Jesus comes in. He took our place by dying for us. Someone has to die for our sins. Either we will, or someone will do it for us. Jesus has already died for us, but for that death to become personal, we must accept what He's done.

Let's get back to Paul. Why was he fortunate? Paul was fortunate because he followed his own advice. He trusted in Christ as his Lord. Paul spoke to Christ about his condition, and we must do the same. We must pray. After all, the Scripture teaches us: "Everyone who calls on the name of the Lord will be saved" (Romans 10:13). We're fortunate if we speak words of confession to God.

the fully devoted life

You may be wondering, what do I say? Say something like this: "Dear God, I know You love me, and I know I don't deserve Your love. I've done things wrong. I've sinned against You. I'm sorry for my failures. I know You sent your Son Jesus to die for me so that I may be forgiven and not be punished for my sin. I thank You, Jesus, for what You've done for me in Your death and resurrection. I trust You, and I ask You to take my sin away, to come into my heart, and to be the Lord of my life. I confess You as Lord. I ask You to help me live for You."

This commitment is like a wedding vow. Before we make vows, we are bride and groom. After the vows, we are wife and husband. What changed? Our commitment to one another changed. The same is true in our relationship with God. Before making our commitment, we were separated from God and had no relationship. After our commitment, we became one in relationship. If you haven't committed your life to Christ and you have a desire to do so, I encourage you to pray a prayer like the one above and mean it with your heart. That prayer will change your life.

We are fortunate that we have a way out.

Paul included these words of Christ. Jesus said, "So that they may receive forgiveness of sins and a place among those who are sanctified by faith in me" (Acts 26:18). Guess what? If you prayed a prayer like the one above to God and meant it, He heard you and said yes to your request. Remember, it's a promise. Not only was Paul fortunate to have a relationship with God, but if you've received forgiveness and committed your life to Christ, then so are you! Your spiritual journey with God has begun.

The first way Paul was fortunate was in knowing God. The second way he considered himself fortunate was in having the opportunity to tell other people about his knowing God. He had a story to tell.

We are fortunate when we can share our faith.

We're fortunate to be able to help people see their sickness. It's awesome to know that we're privileged to help someone notice something they have that's killing them and to tell them about the cure. Let's get personal.

Q: Paul considered himself to be fortunate. Do you feel fortunate that you have a story to tell that can bring change in others? Why?

Q: Are you telling your story? Why or why not?

We can develop our story as we think about what God has done for us. Although the events may be different, there are similarities in what Paul experienced and what we have experienced on our path to God. Let's take some time to get into the specifics of Paul's story and apply it to our own story.

As we think about these things and answer questions about our journey toward discovering God, we begin putting our story together, a story that is meant to be shared.

Sharing my escape story

We need to share with others how our lives were before we met God. We didn't have a relationship with God, and we were separated from Him, like someone in prison is separated from loved ones in the outside world. Paul was literally in prison, but we were in a spiritual place without God. Something put us in that position. What was it?

I was in prison because I supported the wrong thing.

Although Paul had done nothing wrong, we found ourselves in our condition because we did. Paul was in prison because he supported the right thing: God. We were in our condition because we supported the wrong thing. We trusted in something that falls short to give us meaning in life. Something became the object of our desire. It became our god, and it didn't satisfy.

Author and pastor Tim Keller gave a great definition of sin. He wrote, "Sin isn't only doing bad things, it is more fundamentally making good things into ultimate things. Sin is building your life and meaning on anything, even a very good thing, more than on God. Whatever we build our life on will drive us and enslave us. Sin is primarily idolatry."[1] He's right! We make things our idols and support them. That was our problem. We lived for the wrong god.

The truth is that we supported the enemy of God. He has a name: Satan. The Scripture teaches us why Jesus came. He came "to open their eyes and turn them from darkness to light, and from the power of Satan to God" (Acts 26:18).

the fully devoted life

There are not many people who get up in the morning and say "I'm going to live for Satan today." Only Satan worshippers would do something like that. Yet we supported him; he leads people to live for themselves. Doing so becomes the primary concern for many. Their motive is to protect themselves and advance their own cause. They become selfish, believing that they're in control of their destiny and that they have the power to deal with any situation. Sometimes they do so in the name of religion. Paul is a good example. His religion was: "do work so that people respect and honor me." He was concerned about his position, but things changed when he met Christ. He became concerned about how people saw Christ through the way he lived his life.

Before knowing Christ, Paul had strong beliefs about rules, not relationships. Jesus talked about this. He said: "They worship me in vain; their teachings are but rules taught by men" (Mark 7:7). Paul relied on his ability to obey rules for his sense of value. We always fail; therefore we lose our value. A religion about our ability is a religion of self-centeredness. We're trapped by our own self-effort. Paul changed who he supported and found freedom knowing that the One who controls all things was in control of his life.

Q: What did you believe would make you happy? What did you live for?

the fully devoted life

I escaped prison by supporting the right thing.

Not only do we need to share our story about our life before Christ, we also need to share what happened as we came to know Christ. All believers have something in common: we decided to change the object of our trust. We began to trust in Him.

Our support of one thing puts us in opposition against other things. In this case, Paul opposed those who believed in Christ.

> I too was convinced that I ought to do all that was possible to oppose the name of Jesus of Nazareth. And that is just what I did in Jerusalem. On the authority of the chief priests I put many of the saints in prison, and when they were put to death, I cast my vote against them. Many a time I went from one synagogue to another to have them punished, and I tried to force them to blaspheme. In my obsession against them, I even went to foreign cities to persecute them.
>
> Acts 26:9-11

Paul changed his object of trust. Jesus got his attention as he traveled down the road toward Damascus by putting a spotlight on him. Literally, a light from heaven beamed down on him, and his eyes were blinded. He responded to this event. He asked, "Who are you, Lord?" (Acts 9:15). Jesus used this occasion to confront Paul with his behavior. Although he couldn't see with his physical eyes, he could see his spiritual condition. God had exposed Paul's spiritual disease, and he longed to be healed. He trusted in Christ and began living for Him. His life transformed.

Paul asked the question, "Who are you, Lord?" We ask this common question when things happen to wake us up from our current condition. We want to know who's messing with us. Look at the common questions we ask.

the fully devoted life

- "Who are you?" We want to know who is trying to get our attention.
- "What do you want?" We want to know what His expectations are.
- "Are you what I'm looking for?" We're looking for meaning in life. We want to know if He is the One who will provide it.

We've read about Paul's story; what about yours? Take some time to answer the following questions.

Q: What events caused you to want to accept Christ? What did God do to wake you up to see that you needed Him?

Q: When you committed your life to Christ, what did you say to Him?

Q: How has your life been different since you became a Christian?

God, I thank You for reminding me of what You have done in my life to lead me to where I am today. I thank You for getting my attention and showing me Your love, a love that has changed my life forever. Please help me as I share my love story with those who need You.

Chapter Three
The Purpose:
Imagine a life that shares God openly.

> But you will receive power when the Holy Spirit comes on you; and you will be my witnesses in Jerusalem, and in all Judea and Samaria, and to the ends of the earth.
>
> Acts 1:8

What we do for a living affects us in a powerful way. Many find a great deal of their self-worth through their occupation. At one time, this principle was primarily true of men. As time has gone by and as women have become more involved in the work force, we find this principle to be true of both genders. Working is not a foreign concept for us as a people. Most of us recognize that nothing comes for free. For us to have money, we must expend effort. For us to see results, we must work. This rule is also true spiritually.

Hopefully, none of us look at living the Christian life as a job. It's not meant to be that way. However, for us to see results, we must act. With this principle in mind, I want to share with you four spiritual occupations that affect our witness. We need to learn how to do each well so that we may see great results through the power of God's Spirit.

The four occupations of a witness

Let's look at a portion of what Paul wrote once again.

> Then I asked, "Who are you, Lord?" "I am Jesus, whom you are persecuting," the Lord replied. "Now get up and stand on your feet. I have appeared to you to appoint you as a servant and as a witness of what you have seen of me and what I will show you. I will rescue you from your

own people and from the Gentiles. I am sending you to them to open their eyes and turn them from darkness to light, and from the power of Satan to God, so that they may receive forgiveness of sins and a place among those who are sanctified by faith in me." So then, King Agrippa, I was not disobedient to the vision from heaven.

Acts 26:15-19

The Doctor: I bring spiritual healing.

Paul's experience was not only about connecting with Jesus; it was also about what to do afterwards. Jesus appointed him. "Then I asked, 'Who are you, Lord?' 'I am Jesus, whom you are persecuting,' the Lord replied. 'Now get up and stand on your feet. I have appeared to you to appoint you as a servant and as a witness of what you have seen of me and what I will show you" (Acts 26:15-16).

Jesus gave Paul a job, which was first to be a servant. A servant reaches out to people in need and helps to meet those needs. A physician does such work in helping those who are sick. The best doctors:

- Care about those in need.
- Diagnose a patient's need.
- Use their talents to meet the need and do so with passion.
- Celebrate with those who are healed.

Wouldn't you love to have a doctor with these qualities? People who are in spiritual trouble need this type of servant.

Healing comes when we notice those who need our help. We see their spiritual cancer (sin), and we know that they need to become aware of it and want it to be removed. Many don't notice their condition until they receive God's love. After all, we're not concerned about how we affect God until we know that God exists and loves us. He shows His love through a

Christian's sacrifice in reaching out to those who need help. This outreach is the beginning of being the spiritual physician God desires.

Q: Who around you is in need?

Q: When was the last time you met a need? (Share the specifics about what the need was and how you met it.)

Q: Did you share with that person why you met his needs?

The History Teacher: I tell my story.

One subject we learn in high school is history. The past has helped to form our society and world into what it is today amazes me. That same pattern is also true of our spiritual lives. We have a history which has formed us into who we are. Remember, we need to be great storytellers, taking people back in time to help them grasp our experiences.

This need gets us back to what we've learned. You were asked several questions about your life before Christ, how you came to Christ, and how your life has been since knowing Him. Not only do we need to remember what God has done and what He's doing, but we also need to be able to tell our story in an easily understandable way.

We need to practice telling our story. As you practice, you may find yourself using words or phrases that people who are unchurched may not get. Those who grew up in the church share this common problem. We expect others to understand our religious language when they may not have had our same experiences. We need to say what happened in a way that makes sense.

The Marketing Supervisor: I reach a circle of influence.

Jesus sent Paul to a specific group of people to help them see what they really needed. "I will rescue you from your own people and from the Gentiles. I am sending you to them" (Acts 26:17).

God not only appoints us to be a witness, but He also has a target for us to reach. That target is the people within our circles of influence. We see a great example in this Scripture. Jesus talked to Paul about being rescued, but then He told Paul who his target audience was. Jesus was sending Paul to his own people. They were in his circle. He knew them best and knew their needs.

We have the greatest potential to reach those we know because we have a grasp of what we need to communicate the message. To share with them effectively, we have to be a great example. This occupation is called a "marketing supervisor" because a marketing supervisor has someone to whom to market. But this job is not all about the market; it's also about the supervision. We need to supervise our lives. In other words, we need to make sure we have our lives under control so that those in our circles see a good example of who Christ is. Your life is as if Vanna White from *Wheel of Fortune* were standing next to you, flinging her arms in front of you and saying, "And this is what you'll be like if you give your life to Christ." Is your life one that's appealing?

We help those in our market come to know their need for Christ. Think about it: that's what a salesperson does. He finds people who need something and explains to them how what he sells will meet that need. The best salespeople have purchased and used the product themselves. Those who buy or use a competitor's product are terrible examples of why someone should buy something. Why would they sell one product if they're using another?

As believers, we don't market something we haven't bought. Our message has power because we saw the value of knowing Christ and accepted Him. We need to help others see their need for Him.

Who do you know that needs Christ? Who is in your circle of influence? Below, you see a diagram that will help you identify people in your circle who need Jesus. In the center of the illustration, write the word "ME." The circles that move out from the center describe groups of people who are influenced, beginning with those who are closest to you. Listed are family, friends, neighbors, classmates, acquaintances, and people in your traffic pattern. Those in your traffic pattern are people that you see frequently but with whom you don't really have a relationship, maybe the person who works in the cafeteria at your school or who checks you out at the video store.

Answer the questions which appear after the diagram. They relate to those in your circles of influence.

CIRCLES OF INFLUENCE

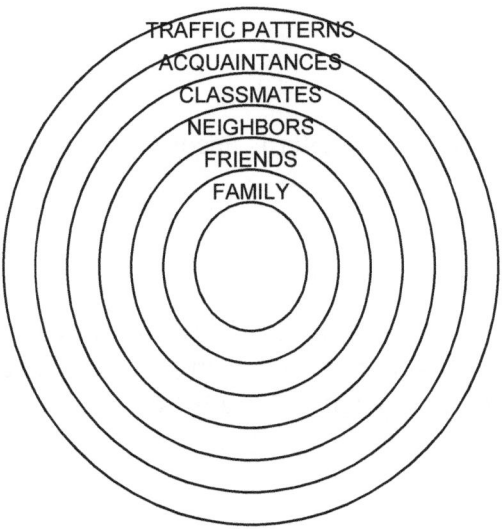

the fully devoted life

Q: Who in your family needs Christ?

Q: Who are your friends who need Christ?

Q: Who in your neighborhood needs Christ?

Q: Who at your school needs Christ?

Q: Who are the people you casually know (acquaintances) who need Christ?

Q: Who in your traffic patterns needs Christ?

Q: Are you a living example of Christ to those in your circles of influence? If you are not an example to all in your circle, write down the group that needs a better example from you.

The names on the previous page are going to be a part of our circle of prayer. Begin praying for each person, asking God to give you opportunities to share your story. Your circle may change. Continue to use this tool as you become aware of others who need a relationship with Christ.

The Optometrist: I correct bad vision.

We are to be spiritual optometrists. Look at what Jesus said: "To open their eyes and turn them from darkness to light, and from the power of Satan to God, so that they may receive forgiveness of sins and a place among those who are sanctified by faith in me" (Acts 26:18). Paul's calling was to help clear up bad vision. He knew what bad vision was all about; after all, Jesus had blinded him. Just as God healed Paul's eyes, he was to open the eyes of those who needed spiritual healing. We see things very differently when our eyes open to God's will. We stop living our lives in darkness and begin living with purpose and joy. Jesus said that Paul was to turn them not only from darkness to light, but also from the power of Satan to the power of God. Think of it this way. We need to change the lens through which we look at our lives. We need God's lens power, not Satan's.

People need to see clearly what procedure will correct their vision of life. We've learned about this operation before. This procedure, called forgiveness, removes the blocker that an eye doctor may call a cataract, but that God calls sin. The sin must be removed. Those who undergo the spiritual surgical procedure of confession:

- know that the spiritual cataract (sin) is there
- know that they put it there
- know that sin needs to be removed
- want their sin to be removed
- tell God they have a problem (go to the doctor)
- ask his assistant, Jesus, to remove it.

the fully devoted life

With our spiritual vision cleared, now we see the world through different eyes. We see the path God wants us to walk, and we begin walking in a different direction. We stop running into things that damage us, avoiding them instead so that we can experience the best life possible.

Often, though, we revert to unhealthy behaviors in which we participated before coming to know Christ. This regression affects our witness in a negative way by once again including things in life that keep us from seeing people in need. We focus on ourselves, and we don't notice what goes on around us. If we live in darkness, helping people see what causes darkness is hard for us.

Speaking openly about God

I will speak openly about God when nothing stands in the way.

Here are some key truths.

- My not sharing openly may reveal that something is in the way.
- I need to see what distracts me away from being concerned about people.
- I need to acknowledge my problem through prayer.
- I need to work to overcome the temptation that leads me to fail.
- I need to be out of control with God, the Lord of my life, in control.

Addressing these issues prepares us to speak the message with strength. We need a pure heart to speak for God. We should pray a prayer like the one that follows. I encourage you to make it your prayer by reading it out loud. Have a picture of God in your mind, and speak these words to Him.

the fully devoted life

"Create in me a pure heart, O God, and renew a steadfast spirit within me. Do not cast me from your presence or take your Holy Spirit from me. Restore to me the joy of your salvation and grant me a willing spirit, to sustain me" (Psalm 51:10-12). The verse that follows this Scripture tells us what will happen when this verse comes true. "Then I will teach transgressors your ways, and sinners will turn back to you" (Psalm 51:13).

Q: What in your life blurs your vision and keeps you from seeing people in need? What sin is causing a problem?

I will speak openly about God when I remember His awesome deeds (Psalm 66:3).

Do you remember the sacrifice Christ made for you? We can't help but be grateful when we do. God established a way for us to remember what He's done through the Lord's Supper, which calls our mind to the greatest love act of all. The Scripture gives us an account of the first time it was taken.

> Then came the day of Unleavened Bread on which the Passover lamb had to be sacrificed. Jesus sent Peter and John, saying, "Go and make preparations for us to eat the Passover." "Where do you want us to prepare for it?" they asked. He replied, "As you enter the city, a man carrying a jar of water will meet you. Follow him to the house that he enters, and say to the owner of the house, 'The Teacher asks: Where is the guest room, where I may eat the Passover with my disciples?' He will show you a large upper room, all furnished. Make preparations there." They left and found things just as Jesus had told them. So they prepared the Passover. When the hour came, Jesus and his

apostles reclined at the table. And he said to them, "I have eagerly desired to eat this Passover with you before I suffer. For I tell you, I will not eat it again until it finds fulfillment in the kingdom of God." After taking the cup, he gave thanks and said, "Take this and divide it among you. For I tell you I will not drink again of the fruit of the vine until the kingdom of God comes." And he took bread, gave thanks and broke it, and gave it to them, saying, "This is my body given for you; do this in remembrance of me." In the same way, after the supper he took the cup, saying, "This cup is the new covenant in my blood, which is poured out for you."

Luke 22:7-20

We should keep in mind what Jesus has done for us as we participate in the Lord's Supper. We also need to partake in the right way. We need to have a pure heart, which allows us to have a clear focus about what we do. This focus brings our minds back to the significance of what God has done for us and should stir within our hearts a desire to speak of Him.

I will speak openly about God when I recognize God's work in my life.

Not only should we think about the past, but we should also think about the present and how it will affect the future. Consider what's going on in your life right now.

Q: What problems are you having?

Q: How do these problems affect how you see God?

"For you, O God, tested us; you refined us like silver" (Psalm 66:10). God allows things in my life to refine me by building my faith. If I see God as after me, as in trying to get me, then I have a bad attitude about Him and won't sing His praise. If I see God as after me, as in trying to catch me when I go astray to show me His love, then I speak of Him with gratitude, knowing that He's working to build my strength. God is our strength trainer.

Have you ever had a physical trainer? If you were sore because of the workout he or she made you do, did you get mad at the trainer? You were probably upset with yourself for getting into a bad physical condition. We should be grateful that they help us get back into shape. The same is true with God. Seeing God as someone who helps us gain spiritual strength and overcome spiritual weakness changes our perspective of Him. Look at what the psalmist wrote. "You let men ride over our heads; we went through fire and water, but you brought us to a place of abundance" (Psalm 66:12).

Remember these things:

- God does what He does to help us become healthy.
- God does what He does to mold us into someone who looks like Christ.
- Having problems shouldn't turn us away from God but to God.

If your struggles move you away from God, you've got the wrong idea of what He's doing. You see the events through the wrong lens, the lens of ease and prosperity instead of the lens of spiritual growth and faith. Becoming a fully devoted follower of Christ requires spiritual growth and faith.

Q: What is your attitude about what God is doing?

the fully devoted life

I will speak openly about God when I paint a picture of His story.

"I will come to your temple with burnt offerings and fulfill my vows to you—vows my lips promised and my mouth spoke when I was in trouble" (Psalm 66:13-14). Satan wants to confuse us about the commitments we made to God. If he can confuse us, he can keep us quiet.

We need to do something to prove that we were serious about what we did. We need to confirm our decisions. The cool thing about obeying God is that every time we do, we confirm that we know Him. The opposite of this is also true. If we don't obey God, Satan uses this disobedience to confuse us about our decision to give our lives to Him. God gave us a way to confirm our relationship with Him in the first thing He wants us to do.

In order to let people know what God has done for us and to let Satan know we meant business when we committed our lives to Christ, we are open about our "God Story" by obeying Him through baptism. We hear this command from Christ. "Therefore go and make disciples of all nations, baptizing them in the name of the Father and of the Son and of the Holy Spirit, and teaching them to obey everything I have commanded you. And surely I am with you always, to the very end of the age" (Matthew 28:19-20).

We should obey everything God has commanded us to do. Those who are baptized know that their commitment is real because they obeyed what God commanded them to do. We easily become confused when we make commitments that we don't prove. Believers who are baptized put action behind their words and acknowledge the faith they've placed in Christ. Satan often successfully confuses us about our decision to give our lives to Christ because we aren't baptized. Satan uses confusion as a tactic to keep us from sharing our story about what God has done for us. The great thing about baptism is that it's one of the first ways we tell our story.

the fully devoted life

Those who are baptized openly witness about what God has done for them. He died for them, was buried for them, and rose so that they may live. Baptism paints the picture of the story of Christ. We symbolize His death when we stand in the water. We symbolize His burial when we lie under the water. We symbolize His resurrection when we come out of the water. We serve a Savior who lives! Say that out loud.

Q: Have you been baptized? If so, write the details about what happened when you were baptized.

Q: If you haven't been baptized, will you commit right now to do it? If so, write, "I commit to obey God and to follow Christ's example through baptism. I will talk to my minister about a time I can be baptized." Go ahead; write it!

I will speak openly about God when I'm prepared for the response.

We see different responses to the message of Christ. I should be prepared for how people react to the message I share. Let's get back to Paul and read part of the story.

At this point Festus interrupted Paul's defense. "You are out of your mind, Paul!" he shouted. "Your great learning is driving you insane." "I am not insane, most excellent Festus," Paul replied. "What I am saying is true and reasonable. The king is familiar with these things, and I can speak freely to him. I am convinced that none of this has escaped his notice, because it was not done in a corner. King Agrippa, do you believe the prophets? I know you do." Then Agrippa said to Paul, "Do you think that in such a short time you can persuade me to be a Christian?" Paul replied, "Short time or long—I pray God that not only you but all who are listening to me today may become what I am, except for these chains." The king rose, and with him the governor and Bernice and those sitting with them. They left the room, and while talking with one another, they said, "This man is not doing anything that deserves death or imprisonment." Agrippa said to Festus, "This man could have been set free if he had not appealed to Caesar."

Acts 26:24-32

Being prepared for how people respond to us when we share our stories helps us overcome fear. We're prepared for what they may say, and we're not caught off guard. People respond to the Good News in different ways, as we see through the story of Paul's conversion. There he was, being confronted because of his faith in Christ. He was being grilled for his beliefs. Paul took this opportunity to share truth with some people who needed to hear it. We notice two in particular, first of all, Festus. He served as governor during the reign of Agrippa. Festus had interest in what Paul was doing because of the threat it posed to his power and his position. Let's look at how he responded to Paul's account of his spiritual journey. We'll call it:

the fully devoted life

> **The "Festus" response**

"At this point Festus interrupted Paul's defense. 'You are out of your mind, Paul!' he shouted. 'Your great learning is driving you insane'" (Acts 26:24). Festus knew that Paul had been exposed to excellent teaching. Instead of believing that this teaching improved Paul's life, Festus believed that Paul had taken his education too far and had dreamed up some insane explanation about the meaning of life. Some people respond to our story in this way, especially those people who rely on reason completely and discount the importance of faith. Let's take a look at the progression of their response.

Hearing

Disbelief
(Festus believed Paul was crazy)

Rejection

Separation

People like Festus hear the truth, filter it through their reasoning system, and believe that what is said cannot be proven logically. Therefore, they discount what is said, thinking that the one sharing the information is out of his mind. This view of what they have heard leads them to reject the information. This rejection has a consequence: continued separation from God. They're still in the fight. They remain on a godless journey. They don't take advantage of this "wake-up call" opportunity. They continue to be in need, but they may not know it. Those who know it wake up and ask questions about God to determine whether or not He is the solution to their problem. We don't need to be afraid of the Festus response. People like Festus respond out of a lack of knowledge without the benefit of our experience. If they had our experience, they'd know we speak truth and are not delusional in our beliefs.

Q: Has anyone ever given you a Festus response? If so, how did you respond?

Q: Were you like Festus before you became a Christian? If so, what caused you to view Christian ideas as crazy?

The Festus response is not the only one. Someone else reacted to Paul's story. We'll call his reaction:

> ➤ **The "Agrippa" response**

Paul now directs the conversation toward King Agrippa, the big cheese! Paul does so by asking him a question. The king meets Paul's question with a question of his own. Look at the Scripture.

> "King Agrippa, do you believe the prophets? I know you do." Then Agrippa said to Paul, "Do you think that in such a short time you can persuade me to be a Christian?"...They left the room, and while talking with one another, they said, "This man is not doing anything that deserves death or imprisonment." Agrippa said to Festus, "This man could have been set free if he had not appealed to Caesar."
>
> Acts 26:27-28, 31-32

the fully devoted life

Paul asked, "Do you believe the prophets?" Why would he ask this? He asked because the prophets prophesied about a Messiah who would come. Paul wanted Agrippa to see that Jesus fulfilled the prophecy of the coming Christ. Paul tried to help the king process what he had learned about the Messiah so that he could see his need. The king was on to him. Agrippa knew exactly what Paul was doing. We know because of Agrippa's response. He asked, "Do you think that in such a short time you can persuade me to be a Christian?"

Notice two things. First of all, Paul didn't have the power to persuade anyone to receive Christ. Only God can convict someone of his condition and help him see his need for forgiveness. We know we have sinned and need forgiveness from God because God reveals our hearts to us. Every Christian experiences this miracle in the salvation process. Second of all, there is the time factor. Agrippa asked if Paul thought he could convince him in a short time. Again, Paul couldn't convince anyone. But God can, and He can do so in a short time. The time depends on how we respond to what God says. Agrippa may have known his need, but he didn't allow God to meet that need. Some are like this. Look at the progression:

Hearing

Belief

Rejection

Separation

He heard the news. Quite possibly, he believed what Paul had said. An indication of his belief is Agrippa's willingness to let Paul go. He heard and believed, but he still rejected. He would be one of those people who say, "I know I need Christ, but the timing just isn't right." Our receiving Christ isn't only about our timing; it's first about God's timing. He has to offer before we can receive. We can't assume that He'll keep offering. After all, there comes a time when you're offered something for the last time because of your continual rejection.

Agrippa heard, believed, and rejected. Because he rejected, he also remained separated. He was in a fight, and he knew it. God fought to help him see how much He loved him. Agrippa fought for control. He loved himself more than he loved God. That issue always arises when we keep control. Don't be afraid of those who give you this response. Know that God is working on their hearts.

Q: Has anyone ever given you an Agrippa response? If so, how did you respond?

Q: Were you like Agrippa before you became a Christian? If so, why did you feel the invitation came at a bad time?

There's another response, the response of the one who told the story. We'll call it:

> **The "Paul" response**

Look at the progression of events.

Hearing

Belief

Acceptance

Connection

Service

Paul heard the news. Remember, he had an eye-opening experience. He had a wake-up call and heard what Jesus said to him. Not only did he hear it, but he also believed what Jesus said and felt bad about his condition. He stopped loving himself more than loving God. Paul was sorry that he hurt God. Those who love themselves aren't sorry that they hurt others. Paul accepted the offer in God's timing. He accepted the forgiveness that Christ offered. He accepted the offer of Christ to be his Savior. His acceptance connected him to God because the acceptance removed what was keeping Paul away from Him: sin. This acceptance led Paul to be in a position to fulfill what God created him to do. God called him to serve and witness, and Paul began serving and witnessing.

If you're a believer, you're fortunate because you're following the path of Paul. Have you made it all the way? You may have heard, believed, accepted, and connected, but are you serving and witnessing? God wants you to take those steps. The fully devoted are open about what God has done in their lives in hopes that their story will lead others to see how **awesome** God is.

the fully devoted life

How have people responded to your message about Christ? Were they like Festus who refused to believe? Were they like Agrippa who believed but wouldn't make a commitment? Were they like Paul who believed and dedicated his life to Christ? Let's do a little exercise. In the space below, write the names of those with whom you've shared Christ in the "Name" column. After dong this, use the words "Festus," "Agrippa," or "Paul" to record their reactions in the "Response" column. Go ahead and get started!

<u>Name</u>   <u>Response</u>

God, thank You for helping me discover those around me who need to hear of You. Please give me the passion and courage to fulfill my role as a witness for You. I offer myself as an instrument for You to use.

Section Three
Time:
A Schedule to Keep

Chapter Four
The Craving:
Imagine a life that hungers for God.

Therefore, rid yourselves of all malice and all deceit, hypocrisy, envy, and slander of every kind. Like newborn babies, crave pure spiritual milk, so that by it you may grow up in your salvation, now that you have tasted that the Lord is good. As you come to him, the living Stone—rejected by men but chosen by God and precious to him—you also, like living stones, are being built into a spiritual house to be a holy priesthood, offering spiritual sacrifices acceptable to God through Jesus Christ.

1 Peter 2:1-5

Have you ever accidentally drunk spoiled milk? It's not very tasty! Spiritually, we can become spoiled milk. We become difficult for others to swallow. This occurs because of the behaviors we perform. We aren't loving, we're hateful. Are you spoiled milk?

Getting rid of what spoils my milk.

What's spoiling us? What do we absorb that causes our lives to be difficult for others to receive? What influences are ruining us? There are areas of struggle that affect our ability to see others the way God wants and present God in a way He desires. We need to do something about this, but first we need to know what they are.

Knowing what spoils my life.

We should rid ourselves of things that cause people to reject God. Peter lists several.

- **Malice**

What is it? Malice is a desire to cause others pain and suffering because of our feelings about their behavior.

Max Lucado, in *The Applause of Heaven*, wrote about a man named Daniel whose brother had cheated him out of money. He made a vow that he would break his brother's neck if he ever saw him again. God did something amazing in his life. He revealed Himself to Daniel, who became a Christian. Still, Daniel continued to struggle with a heart of bitterness, finding it difficult to forgive his brother. The big moment came when he saw his brother on a busy street. What would he do? He described the event this way:

> "I saw him, but he didn't see me. I felt my fists clench and my face get hot. My initial impulse was to grab him around the throat and choke the life out of him. But as I looked into his face, my anger began to melt. For as I saw him, I saw the image of my father. I saw my father's eyes. I saw my father's look. I saw my father's expression. And as I saw my father in his face, my enemy once again became my brother."

His brother didn't feel Daniel's hands around his neck; he felt his arms around his body as he gave him a big hug. There they were among the people on the street having their very own love fest. His enemy once again became his brother.[3] Instead of harming him, Daniel became a living example of Christ by forgiving him.

Q: If you have a desire to inflict pain on someone, what has he done to deserve it?

- **Deceit**

What is it? We distort the truth to mislead others in an effort to harm them or to gain something personally. We may cheat them out of something or commit fraud, taking advantage of them for personal gain.

Q: If you're deceiving someone, why are you doing it?

- **Hypocrisy**
What is it? We say something about ourselves that we prove false through our behavior.

Q: If you have been a hypocrite, what have you been doing that goes against what you've been saying about God?

- **Envy**
What is it? We are not content, and we covet what someone else has, whether it's possessions, position, or power.

Q: If you are envious, what is it that you want that others have?

- **Slander**

What is it? We tear people down to elevate our own status, making it appear that we are right and they are wrong.

Q: If you slander others, what have they done to deserve your talking to them in an unkind way?

Knowing why these things become a part of my life.

These qualities become a part of life because of wrong cravings. We expose ourselves to things we shouldn't consume and they begin affecting us in a negative way. The things of the world begin to appeal to our appetites. They lead us to be self-centered which results in our harming others in order to protect ourselves. The goal, if we give in to unhealthy things, is to change the craving of our spiritual appetites. We need to crave what God offers. We must begin to take in the things of God and discard the temptations of the world by avoiding them.

Our behavior indicates the appetite of our hearts. If we are loving, it comes from healthy spiritual nutrition. If we are hateful, it comes from unhealthy spiritual nutrition. Which behavior most often exposes you when you take in wrong nutrition? Is it malice, deceit, hypocrisy, envy, or slander? Answer the following question.

Q: Which of these do you struggle with the most?

Q: Why do you think you struggle with this?

Craving something new

If we've been longing for things that are unhealthy, we need to begin craving something new. We've been looking at the old menu, the things we involved ourselves in prior to our commitments to Christ. We need a new menu.

Craving what tastes good

What do you crave? The scripture tells us that we are to crave pure spiritual milk. We are to crave things that bring us good spiritual health. We should desire to surround ourselves with good influences that lead us to take on the look of Christ. They give us a pure example and are pure spiritual milk.

There are times that pure spiritual milk, things that make us healthy, comes in the form of tough love. We may receive a message or experience a circumstance that is difficult in order to bring a positive result. It's done to bring correction. We often want to avoid this because we don't believe it will taste good. We know we need it because it's good for us, but we don't want it because it's not appealing. It may not be appealing, but when it's covered with love, it's awesome going down making its way right into our hearts. Love beats cheese or chocolate any day of the week.

Craving the right life

We often think about the good life as a life full of happiness or a life of freedom with enough money to buy what we want and to go where we want. Peter didn't teach about that kind of good life. He wrote, "Live such good lives among the pagans that, though they accuse you of doing wrong, they may see your good deeds and glorify God on the day he visits us" (1 Peter 2:12). It's cool to know that we can experience a good life in the face of conflict and confrontation. Our happiness isn't dependent on how people treat us. Those who come against us need the life we have to offer. Their hatred needs to be met with our love. We should crave a life like this. We should desire to live like this. When we do, we expose a life that is fully committed to Christ. We make a positive difference. The real good life is the life that has a positive impact. Living it has an affect on both us and others.

The good life is the:
- **Feel Good Life**. It begins with feeling good about life. We feel good about our lives when we feel significant. We all look for significance, which we feel when we are loved. Feeling good about life is the foundation for doing good things in life – things that positively affect others. Those who live the **feel good life** live the...
- **Blame Free Life**. Those who live the blame free life aren't to blame for spreading spiritual disease. They don't live as spoiled milk. If we're spoiled milk, we lead others to be spiritually unhealthy. We're to blame. If we're not spoiled milk, no one can blame us for bad things happening in the world. No one can rightly accuse us of influencing others to make bad decisions. Those who live the **blame free life** live the....
- **Guilt Free Life**. We have no reason to feel guilty because we've done nothing to encourage bad behavior. Peter wrote about pagans who accuse us of doing wrong. Being accused of doing wrong doesn't mean we have done

wrong. However, if we have done wrong, it doesn't feel good. Kiss the good life goodbye. Knowing that we caused other people harm doesn't feel good. The guilt sets in. Sometimes our bad decisions affect people mentally, emotionally, physically, and socially. Most importantly, our bad decisions can lead others to be affected in a negative way spiritually. If we live the **guilt free** life, we know we are living the…

- **Positive influence life.** We're encouraging others to live the good life.

Q: Are you living the good life? If not, why?

Craving what causes growth

There is something true of all babies. They need nourishment to grow, and that nourishment comes from milk. We've been learning about pure spiritual milk, which is what we must begin to crave if we're to grow into the people who live the good life: one that is fully devoted to God. This pure spiritual milk comes not only from positive examples, but also from the instruction we receive from God's Word.

Think about babies again. As they grow, they are expected to reach certain levels in their growth that relate to such things as weight and motor skills. They're expected to reach these goals within certain time periods. They need to meet them to be able to fight infection and those things that can cause physical harm. The same is true of believers. God expects growth, and if we don't meet certain expectations, we aren't healthy. We are subject to disease, which can lead us to experience spiritual illness. God doesn't specify when these expectations are to be met. He sets no certain time period, but

He does expect us to begin making changes in our lives to begin the process of growth.

Q: What are you doing to take in pure spiritual milk (His instruction that leads to growth)?

Q: Are you meeting God's expectations of spiritual growth?

Seeing myself as a construction site

Let's think of ourselves in another way. The following Scripture lays a foundation of an important way to see our spiritual journey. Look again at verses 4-5. "As you come to him, the living Stone—rejected by men but chosen by God and precious to him— you also, like living stones, are being built into a spiritual house to be a holy priesthood, offering spiritual sacrifices acceptable to God through Jesus Christ" (1 Peter 2:4-5).

God liked what He saw, and so He picked me to be a place of construction. The Scripture teaches us that we are chosen. God chooses us because we are precious to Him. Those who recognize God's desire for us and know His love come alive. God uses these alive people to build His church. God wants us to focus on certain aspects so that we can build in a way that makes a difference. What should we look like? We've already learned this. We are to look like Jesus! Let's give a name to what God is creating. That finished product is what we'll call a spiritual house.

There are times that people who are looking for a new house take tours of model homes. Many find the house they like and have one built just like it. They copy it. What does this example have to do with our spiritual condition? Good question! The answer is simple: would anyone want to copy you? People look for those after whom they can model their lives. How about you?

Q: If you were a house, would anyone want to build a house like you? Why?

Winning the war

Dear friends, I urge you, as aliens and strangers in the world, to abstain from sinful desires, which war against your soul. Live such good lives among the pagans that, though they accuse you of doing wrong, they may see your good deeds and glorify God on the day he visits us.

1 Peter 2:11-12

The war of desire

  We become like Christ when we desire to do so. Becoming is all about passion. Action and passion go together. We may go into action without passion, but we don't have passion without going into action. We may be made to do something, but with passion, we want to do something. The more passion we have, the more we do to achieve the goal. Again, the goal is to be like Christ. Our passion grows the more we spend time with God. If we have wrong passions, our spending time with God helps to redirect the desires of our hearts. We're in a desire war. Our sinful desires war with the Savior's. "Therefore, if anyone is in Christ, he is a new creation; the old has gone, the new has come!" (2 Corinthians 5:17). We throw out those things that keep us from full devotion and add things that lead us to be fully devoted. I make sure I don't put myself in a position to be tempted to lose the desire war. Satan wants to bring things our way that influence us to have the wrong desire. He also wants us to feel defeated, without hope of overcoming those things that keep us from honoring God.
  Some people don't believe we can overcome our problems. Chuck Colson wrote about what some leaders in the Seattle Downtown Emergency Services Center believe concerning alcoholics and their ability to overcome their addiction. They're spending $11 million on permanent housing on homeless alcoholics because they're tired of the $50,000 a year they spend on programs that relate to them such as emergency room visits, prison, and recovery programs. They're building the facility to house seventy-five people who will be allowed to drink all they want and aren't required to be in any kind of recovery program. Why? The executive director Bill Hobson believes that once you're an alcoholic, you're always an alcoholic who can't overcome the addiction.[4] He's forgotten one thing: God can transform a life! He can help us overcome worldly desires by replacing them

with a strong passion that leads us into action that honors Him. We can win the war.

The war of liberation

This war is not only about our problems. We fight to liberate people, to help free them from sin (1 Peter 2:12). We're back to the good life again, the one that's blameless and guilt free and has a positive influence on those who are searching for answers. The good life doesn't come on its own; it takes work and dedication.

Q: What desires do you have that need to change?

Q: How much time are you willing to commit to make the needed changes?

God, I thank You for showing me areas in my life that are spoiled. I ask You to give me a new craving, a craving for You.

Chapter Five
The Disciplines:
Imagine a life that manages its opportunities.

The proverbs of Solomon son of David, king of Israel: for attaining wisdom and discipline; for understanding words of insight; for acquiring a disciplined and prudent life, doing what is right and just and fair; for giving prudence to the simple, knowledge and discretion to the young—let the wise listen and add to their learning, and let the discerning get guidance—for understanding proverbs and parables, the sayings and riddles of the wise. The fear of the LORD is the beginning of knowledge, but fools despise wisdom and discipline.

Proverbs 1:1-7

Living a consistent Christian life doesn't happen by accident; it requires discipline. The disciplined life is the wise life, and we show wisdom when we spend time making sure our desires are right. We learned about the life we are to live in the previous chapter. Developing this life requires much effort on our part. We're willing to give this time and to practice the disciplines of our faith if being fully devoted to Christ is our goal and desire. People should be able to tell we're fully devoted followers of Christ. They should see it through how we live and what we communicate.

A Jewish economist named Arthur Burns was very influential in Washington for many years. He once attended an event with several politicians of the evangelical faith. When he was asked to pray, he surprised the audience with his words. He prayed, "Lord, I pray that Jews would come to know Jesus Christ. And I pray that Buddhists would come to know Jesus Christ. And I pray that Muslims would come to know Jesus Christ." He then shocked them all by praying:

"And Lord, I pray that Christians would come to know Jesus Christ."[5]

We all need to know Jesus better. Unfortunately, many don't prove that they know Him at all. Our responsibility as Christians is to live up to the name of Christ. How do I do so?

Living on purpose

The actions of our lives determine our fate. We have a bearing on who we will become and the type of influence we will have. So, we must envision who God wants us to be. Looking into the future, we need to see what living fully for Christ looks like. The decisions we make today must help us reach the goals before us. Our purpose is to live up to that vision. We don't need to live "on accident," just letting things fall where they may; we need to live "on purpose," knowing that God has created us to be a significant part of His plan. Working toward living life a certain way requires effort on our parts. Let's learn about the lives we are to live.

The Regulated Life = The Disciplined Life.

The regulated life is the disciplined life. We control how we live, and so we need to regulate our time to make sure we're giving the relationship we have with God the time that it deserves. We can't expect an awesome relationship with God if we don't engage Him in conversation and learn from Him. God wants us to learn how to live the regulated life!

Q: How much time do you spend with God each day?

the fully devoted life

The Managed Life = The Prudent Life.

God expects us to manage our lives. We specifically must manage the affairs of our lives, including our family, our work, and our finances. We should watch over and organize what God gives us to steward. If we aren't wise, we blow what God gives us and go bankrupt. Some manage their lives, but they do so without God. They're left wanting more.

Tom Brady, one of the most successful quarterbacks in NFL history, still plays the game. In the 2007-2008 season, he set the record for the most touchdown passes in the regular season and won the MVP award. He had already won three Super Bowls by the age of thirty. In 2005, a journalist named Steve Kroft from *60 Minutes* interviewed Tom Brady about his career. Although Brady has succeeded professionally, he expressed his desire for more out of life. He said, "Why do I have three Super Bowl rings and still think there's something greater out there for me? I mean, maybe a lot of people would say, 'Hey man, this is what [it's all about].' I reached my goal, my dream, my life. Me? I think, 'It's got to be more than this.' I mean this isn't—this can't be—all it's cracked up to be." Kroft then asked Brady what the right answer was, and Brady added: "What's the answer? I wish I knew... I love playing football, and I love being quarterback for this team. But at the same time, I think there are a lot of other parts about me that I'm trying to find."[6]

God doesn't want life to be this way. He wants us to experience a full life, and we achieve that life in complete devotion to Him. Our devoted lives are different; we live in a different way. God wants us to learn how to live the managed life!

Q: How well do you manage your time?

Q: What do you need to do to change the way you manage your time?

The Proper Life = The Right Life.

God wants us to learn to live the proper life. The word *proper* means "to conform to an approved standard." We conform to God's standard so that we can distinguish between what is right and wrong. Solomon, who took over the kingdom of Israel at a young age, knew the importance of being able to make wise decisions. He asked: "So give your servant a discerning heart to govern your people and to distinguish between right and wrong. For who is able to govern this great people of yours?" (1 Kings 3:9).

Discerning people are sensitive to what God wants. Being discerning depends on knowing the principles by which God wants us to live. We follow the principles of life that He gives us, and these principles give us something by which to measure our decisions. We ask ourselves four questions when making decisions.

- **What do I want?** "Many are the plans in a man's heart, but it is the LORD'S purpose that prevails" (Proverbs 19:21)

- **What does God want?** Some never get this far. They never ask this question because they're not thinking about God. The fully devoted believer asks this question before "what do I want?" Asking the question "What does God want" first shows that we are becoming fully devoted followers of Christ. Our desires should match God's.

- **Do I want to do what God wants?** We may not want to do what God wants because we know what it will require, perhaps hard circumstances or a change in our lifestyle. This knowledge leads to a decision time. Here's the deal. Our decision may not only affect our fate, but it may also affect the fate of someone else. Keeping this possibility in mind leads to the next question.

- **Am I willing to do what God wants?** If the result is worthwhile, then we're willing. If the result is worthless, we aren't. Serving God is always worthwhile!

The proper life knows what God wants and does what God wants because of a passion for God to be successful. He wants us to learn how to live the proper life.

Q: Which question do you ask first: "what do I want?" or "what does God want?" Why?

The Moral Life = The Just Life.

To be moral is to live by the standard that we know is right. God has wired us to know the difference between right and wrong. For example, no one has to teach you that murder or rape is wrong. We know they're wrong because they hurt others. How our actions affect others determines much of our morality. Harmful actions defy God's moral code. He is love, and He longs to protect and serve, not to use and abuse. It's cool that science tells us this very thing.

The Yale University Infant Cognition Center conducted tests which found that babies as young as six to ten months old know what's right and wrong. Researchers set babies in front of a roller coaster-like track to watch a cartoon-eyed wooden toy try to climb its way to the top of one of the hills. As the toy climbed, other toys came along designed either to help it over the hump or to push it backwards like a bully. When babies then had the opportunity to play with any of the toys on the track, nearly all infants chose the toys that helped and turned their backs on the bullies. They demonstrated their knowledge of appropriate and inappropriate behavior. This knowledge wasn't taught; it was reflex, a part of what they knew to be right and wrong.[7] God wants us to learn how to live the moral life!

Q: Do you regularly misbehave? If so, what are you doing about it?

The Honest Life = The Fair Life.

The Scripture deals with being fair. We're to live this type of life. The fair can take an honest look at themselves, at someone else, and at the situation, and then make a judgment that is impartial toward the person but partial towards God. We are partial toward God because we want His will to be achieved. We use the moral code that is in us to make helpful decisions for those involved in the situation. The partial show favoritism, which helps one person while hurting the other. God wants us to learn how to live the honest life!

the fully devoted life

Q: Do you treat people fairly, or do you play favorites? If you play favorites, why do you do so?

The Observant Life = The Discerning Life.

We need to learn to observe, which means to come to know, to recognize, and to notice what's going on around us. We gain wisdom from seeing how people deal with situations. We learn in a positive or negative way depending on who we begin to imitate. We should imitate those who imitate Christ. "Be imitators of God, therefore, as dearly loved children and live a life of love, just as Christ loved us and gave himself up for us as a fragrant offering and sacrifice to God" (Ephesians 5:1-2)

We are supposed to observe, but people also observe us. Thomas Friedman, a syndicated *New York Times* columnist, devoted a column to the role technology has in daily life. Friedman wrote that technology allows all of us to be a part of the paparazzi. With only a cell phone, we become instant informers. If we include what we've recorded on YouTube, we're an instant star. Not only can we catch the behavior of others, but they can catch ours. All it takes is one wrong move to ruin our reputation. Friedman quoted author Dov Seidman, who wrote, "We don't live in glass houses (houses have walls); we live on glass microscope slides... visible and exposed to all."[8] This statement is so true! We live under a microscope, and people watch us. We must ask the question: "When I'm under the microscope, do people see Jesus living in me?" God wants us to live the observant life!

Q: Who do you watch?

Q: Do you imitate their behavior? Why or why not?

the fully devoted life

Practicing to become perfect

"Practice makes perfect." This maxim reminds me of Larry Bird, the famous Celtics basketball player. He was an incredible example of someone who practiced diligently to be prepared for the game. He wanted the ball when the game was on the line because he believed he was ready to make the game winning shot. He proved through his diligent efforts to prepare a belief that practice makes perfect.

As believers, we need to practice so that we can be perfect. We practice spiritual disciplines that improve our spiritual stamina and teach us to be more Christlike in character. These practices help us live regulated, managed, proper, moral, honest, and observant lives. Our improved character leads to godly action. Those who practice to become perfect become good examples for others to follow as they progress toward Christlikeness. But practice means nothing without application. Let's take some time to learn about some important disciplines that can make a huge difference.

Prayer: The Talk Discipline

When do you pray? Many people pray only in times of crisis, when they need help. Although the midst of a crisis is a great time to pray, it shouldn't be the only time we pray. Our time spent communicating with God forms an important part of our spiritual growth. We can learn so much about our spiritual condition by listening to what we say to God. What do you say when you pray? How do you treat God as you converse with Him? Do you talk to Him as a father and friend or as someone you barely know?

Prayer can be effective if certain aspects appear in our prayer lives. To teach these aspects, let's look at an acrostic for the word *prayer*.

- **P = Passion**. The passion we have for God affects our prayer life. The more passionate we are, the more intimate the conversation. The less passionate we are, the more we talk to God like an acquaintance rather than a father and friend. If we are passionate for Him, we pray in the right way. The Scripture teaches us how to pray and the results of our prayers when we pray in this manner. "If my people, who are called by my name, will humble themselves and pray and seek my face and turn from their wicked ways, then will I hear from heaven and will forgive their sin and will heal their land" (2 Chronicles 7:14). We see a prayer formula within this Scripture. Check it out!

Humble + Seek + Turn = Hear + Forgive + Heal

The proper attitude is a humble attitude, one that knows God's power and puts Him first. A humble attitude seeks what He wants and turns away from those things that do not please Him. We become aware of what displeases God as we pray. If we pray in humility, God hears us, forgives us, and heals us. He hears the words we speak out of our desire for Him. He forgives us of the things from which we need to turn away. He heals the relationship by strengthening the connection we have with Him. God hears, forgives, and heals through prayer.

Q: Do you talk to God as a Father and friend or as someone you hardly know?

- **R = Recognition**. We recognize who we are by taking an honest look at ourselves. Gary Thomas in *The Beautiful Fight* tells the story of a businessman who became tired of the way people treated him. Customers yelled at him, treating him as if he had no value at all. One day, on the receiving end of yet another yelling attack by a customer, his mind wandered, and he began feeling as though he were watching a movie. The woman was so animated that she looked like she was the staring monkey in the film. This image gave him an idea. He decided to hang a huge mirror right behind the front desk. What happened was amazing. The customers' anger explosions stopped. They couldn't stand how they looked while they acted in a rude manner. When they saw themselves, the screaming ceased.[9] This self-recognition can happen through our prayer lives. Through prayer, we reflect on our condition and begin to see ourselves through God's eyes. We tend to become concerned about how He sees us as we communicate with Him. Our prayer time is a great time to check out our attitudes to see if we live a life that honors Him.

Q: What has God been teaching you through your prayer life?

- **A = Acknowledge**. We tell God about our condition. Our thoughts go to those things that we have done wrong, and we confess them before Him. The knowledge of how our behavior has affected Him in a negative way makes us sorry for what we've done to Him and the relationship we have with Him.

Q: Have you been honest with God about your spiritual life? What have you said to Him?

- **Y = Yield**. We agree with God about how He sees our behavior, and we become willing to make changes to honor Him. We learned that turning is a part of the effective prayer. Saying that we're sorry is not enough; we need to prove that we're sorry. The truth is that God knows if we're sorry, because He knows our heart. He knows if our behavior will change. However, our change of behavior proves to ourselves the commitment we have toward Him. We need to say **yes** to Him in our prayer. We need to say **yes** to His plan of correction.

Q: Have you agreed with God about His opinion of who you are spiritually? If so, what are you willing to do to change His opinion?

- **E = Express**. After coming clean about our condition, we are now in a place of purity, and we can offer praise to God without any hindrance. Now is time to honor Him for who He is. God is our Creator who is **awesome** in love and power.

Q: What reasons do you have to praise God?

- **R = Return**. We commit ourselves to His plan for living. We took a wrong turn, and we returned to the path He wants us to travel. We commit ourselves to stay on that path, follow Him as Lord, and ask Him to help us as we live.

Q: Is God the Lord (ruler) of your life? Why or why not?

Prayer is one important discipline. We also need to practice the discipline of study as we dig into God's Word. Let's learn about this discipline.

Study: The Listen Discipline

We learn about the importance of learning from God through young King Solomon. We read a part of this passage earlier; now let's take a closer look.

> Solomon answered, "You have shown great kindness to your servant, my father David, because he was faithful to you and righteous and upright in heart. You have continued this great kindness to him and have given him a son to sit on his throne this very day. Now, O LORD my God, you have made your servant king in place of my father David. But I am only a little child and do not know how to carry out my duties. Your servant is here among the people you have chosen, a great people, too numerous to count or number. So give your servant a discerning heart to govern your people and to distinguish between right and wrong. For who is able to govern this great people of yours?" The Lord was pleased that Solomon had asked for this. So God said to him, "Since you have asked for this and not for long life or wealth for yourself, nor have asked for the death of your enemies but for discernment in administering justice, I will do what you have asked. I will give you a wise and discerning heart, so that there will never have been anyone like you, nor will there ever be.
>
> 1 Kings 3:6-12

We become interested in what God says when we know we need His advice. Solomon was definitely in that place. When he took over as the king of Israel, he knew he needed help. We should be like Solomon, who knew he needed wisdom, asked for it, received it, and followed it.

Q: In what areas of your life do you need God's advice?

Q: When did you last ask for God's advice? Why?

Q: What did God reveal to you?

Q: Have you followed God's instruction?

Gaining this wisdom requires study. Paul wrote these words of instruction to Timothy: "Study to show thyself approved unto God, a workman that needeth not to be ashamed, rightly dividing the word of truth" (2 Timothy 2:15 KJV). We study so that God approves of us. God approves of us when we live up to His expectations, and we learn what they are through study. Those who know what to do and do what they should have no reason to be ashamed. If we don't take time to learn from Him, we become ashamed because we've wasted time that we could have used to get to know Him better and serve Him. Let's take a look at some important parts of this discipline by looking at the acrostic for the word *study*.

- **S = Sight**. We open our eyes to see what God wants to reveal to us.

> And this is my prayer: that your love may abound more and more in knowledge and depth of insight, so that you may be able to discern what is best and may be pure and blameless until the day of Christ, filled with the fruit of righteousness that comes through Jesus Christ—to the glory and praise of God.
> Philippians 1:9-11

God begins to teach us about what we should include in our lives, things that lead us to look like Christ. We grow in resemblance to Jesus when our devotion to Him grows in every area of life. We need to see what He wants us to become. Those who experience full devotion begin seeing the world through His eyes.

Q: Why is seeing the world through God's eyes important for you?

- **T = Time**. We spend time learning from God. We expose ourselves to His teachings through times of corporate worship, Bible study in smaller groups, and one-on-one time with Him. We commit a portion of our day to improve our relationship with God by allowing Him to teach us what we need to know. We allow God to speak to us.

Q: How much time do you spend during the day reading the Bible?

- **U = Understanding**. We seek to grasp what God says to us. We compare His Word to our lives to understand our true condition. We also take time to gain more instruction if we don't understand what God's Word says to us. Gaining understanding is an important exercise which can be accomplished by learning from other believers through a lesson (sermon), in a one on one setting, in a small group, or through books written by Christian authors.

Q: How does your life compare to what God wants you to be?

Q: If you've had small group study experiences, how has it helped you understand God's Word?

- **D = Dedication**. We commit ourselves to following the plan He has revealed to us. This dedication gets back to Solomon. Not only did he know he needed wisdom and ask for it, but when he received it, he followed it. Following God's instruction doesn't mean he was always perfect and obedient. But Solomon knew the importance of listening to God and doing what He said.

Q: How committed are you to following God's plan for your life?

- **Y = Yielding**. We use information that we receive to make decisions. We ask, "What is God's desire?" To be obedient and prove our wisdom, we yield to Him by saying yes to His plan. Remember, we first ask, "What does God want me to do?"

the fully devoted life

Q: What questions do you ask yourself before making a decision?

Planning: The Doing Discipline

At the beginning of this book you were given Scriptures and a format to have a daily time with God. Be honest: have you been doing so? Have you been spending time daily in His Word and praying to Him? If not, it's catch-up time. If you've been keeping up, keep it up!

The format that was given to you to do your daily quiet time is a good one to continue to practice after you complete this book. Purchase a notebook or journal and keep spending time with God in an intimate setting, getting to know Him better. This habit is an important part of our daily routine. Spending time with God can radically change your attitude and your life. Don't give up! This habit is worth your time.

We should deliberately provide time to spend with God. In our busy schedules, the time we need with Him slips away easily. When is the best time for you to spend in one-on-one time with Him? Fill your schedule on the following pages with routine events like school, school clubs, sports or other regular activities. You'll notice that the time periods are for the entire day; so don't forget to block out time for sleep. What about the spiritual stuff? For right now, let's concentrate on your church activities, like worship, small group, or ministries in which you're involved. If you have already planned a personal time with God, go ahead and note it. You may want to use a highlighter to highlight the time you're spending on your spiritual life. It's time to get started!

The Daily Planner

Time	MONDAY
12:00 am	
1:00	
2:00	
3:00	
4:00	
5:00	
6:00	
7:00	
8:00	
9:00	
10:00	
11:00	
12:00 pm	
1:00	
2:00	
3:00	
4:00	
5:00	
6:00	
7:00	
8:00	
9:00	
10:00	
11:00	

Time	TUESDAY
12:00 am	
1:00	
2:00	
3:00	
4:00	
5:00	
6:00	
7:00	
8:00	
9:00	
10:00	
11:00	
12:00 pm	
1:00	
2:00	
3:00	
4:00	
5:00	
6:00	
7:00	
8:00	
9:00	
10:00	
11:00	

Time	WEDNESDAY
12:00 am	
1:00	
2:00	
3:00	
4:00	
5:00	
6:00	
7:00	
8:00	
9:00	
10:00	
11:00	
12:00 pm	
1:00	
2:00	
3:00	
4:00	
5:00	
6:00	
7:00	
8:00	
9:00	
10:00	
11:00	

Time	THURSDAY
12:00 am	
1:00	
2:00	
3:00	
4:00	
5:00	
6:00	
7:00	
8:00	
9:00	
10:00	
11:00	
12:00 pm	
1:00	
2:00	
3:00	
4:00	
5:00	
6:00	
7:00	
8:00	
9:00	
10:00	
11:00	

Time	FRIDAY
12:00 am	
1:00	
2:00	
3:00	
4:00	
5:00	
6:00	
7:00	
8:00	
9:00	
10:00	
11:00	
12:00 pm	
1:00	
2:00	
3:00	
4:00	
5:00	
6:00	
7:00	
8:00	
9:00	
10:00	
11:00	

Time	SATURDAY
12:00 am	
1:00	
2:00	
3:00	
4:00	
5:00	
6:00	
7:00	
8:00	
9:00	
10:00	
11:00	
12:00 pm	
1:00	
2:00	
3:00	
4:00	
5:00	
6:00	
7:00	
8:00	
9:00	
10:00	
11:00	

Time	SUNDAY
12:00 am	
1:00	
2:00	
3:00	
4:00	
5:00	
6:00	
7:00	
8:00	
9:00	
10:00	
11:00	
12:00 pm	
1:00	
2:00	
3:00	
4:00	
5:00	
6:00	
7:00	
8:00	
9:00	
10:00	
11:00	

Now that you see your schedule, if you don't already have a one-on-one time with God, what time do you have to spend with Him? Maybe you need to rearrange some things so that you can have a consistent time. Once you schedule those times, you may want to go back and highlight them. You have a schedule. Congratulations. Keep it!

God, I want to spend time with You! I ask you to speak to me and train me to be devoted in all areas of my life. Thank You for wanting to have a relationship with someone who is imperfect and flawed. You are my God, and I want to learn from You.

Section Four
Talents:
The Gifts to Use

Chapter Six
The Passion:
Imagine a life that exercises concern for others.

Therefore, since Christ suffered in his body, arm yourselves also with the same attitude, because he who has suffered in his body is done with sin. As a result, he does not live the rest of his earthly life for evil human desires, but rather for the will of God. For you have spent enough time in the past doing what pagans choose to do—living in debauchery, lust, drunkenness, orgies, carousing and detestable idolatry. They think it strange that you do not plunge with them into the same flood of dissipation, and they heap abuse on you. But they will have to give account to him who is ready to judge the living and the dead. For this is the reason the gospel was preached even to those who are now dead, so that they might be judged according to men in regard to the body, but live according to God in regard to the spirit. The end of all things is near. Therefore be clear minded and self-controlled so that you can pray. Above all, love each other deeply, because love covers over a multitude of sins. Offer hospitality to one another without grumbling. Each one should use whatever gift he has received to serve others, faithfully administering God's grace in its various forms. If anyone speaks, he should do it as one speaking the very words of God. If anyone serves, he should do it with the strength God provides, so that in all things God may be praised through Jesus Christ. To him be the glory and the power for ever and ever. Amen.

                                              1 Peter 4:1-11

Having the same attitude as Christ

"Therefore, since Christ suffered in his body, arm yourselves also with the same attitude, because he who has suffered in his body is done with sin" (1 Peter 4:1). My passion has everything to do with my attitude, and I need to have the attitude of Christ if I am going to be fully devoted to Him. The attitude of Christ is the attitude of sacrifice. Our attitude is a weapon. The Scripture teaches us that we arm ourselves with His attitude. We use this weapon to defeat hatred. Love trumps the hatred which comes against us.

People need to know they are loved. Love begins with the attitude we have toward them. Our service to others has everything to do with how we see them. We ask ourselves the question: are they worth it? The answer to that question is always **yes**, but we may not come to that conclusion. We may feel that they aren't worth it. Aren't you glad that Jesus didn't feel that way about you?

Our attitude toward others affects how much we're willing to sacrifice. This principle is really important, because we are supposed to sacrifice enough for them to know they are loved. The problem comes when our sacrifice falls short. It's not enough. We should be willing to give everything to help people know they are valuable. Jesus made a powerful statement when He said: "My command is this: Love each other as I have loved you. Greater love has no one than this, that he lay down his life for his friends" (John 15:12-13).

Our service can make a difference. Christine Bouwkamp and Kyle Kramer believed in the power of sacrifice. They wanted to approach their wedding in a way that could make a difference. Rather than having the typical reception after the ceremony, they decided to do something they believed would have more significance. They invited the guests who came to the wedding to join them in helping to distribute food to people in the area who were in need. They did so because they wanted to begin their marriage with an act of sacrifice and service to Christ.

To have the resources to provide the food, they determined how much money they would have spent on the reception and dedicated those funds toward the cost of food. The money purchased five thousand pounds. During the week of the wedding, they put out the word into the community that free food would be available at the church immediately after they shared their vows. As a result, because of their service, one hundred families experienced the love of Christ shown to them through their service and sacrifice.[10]

Q: What sacrifices do you make for others?

Q: Are those sacrifices enough for them to see the love of God?

Living with the right motivation

"As a result, he does not live the rest of his earthly life for evil human desires, but rather for the will of God" (1 Peter 4:2). What are you trying to accomplish with your life? Make a decision about how you're going to live the rest of your life. Live it on purpose to accomplish God's will. What is God's will? He wants us to live up to our calling. Be motivated to live up to that calling. If you're not, you stall. Your engine sputters, and you don't do the things you should to impact the world. Live in such a way that the world buys in to God's love.

Do you love buying things? There are different types of buyers. Some are impulse buyers who buy without thinking, and some are process buyers who buy after processing the

the fully devoted life

impact of the purchase. No matter what type of buyer you are, you connect with the product before you purchase it.

We see products in plenty of ways these days because advertising is such a big deal in our society. A seller's goal is to get us emotionally involved in his product. He does so by connecting our senses to what he's selling. We see the product. If it looks good, we begin to imagine what our lives would be like if we had it. We touch it. Touch is huge in the sales world. If we can feel it, we have a greater sense of ownership. We smell it. Smell may or may not be a big deal depending on the product. Put people in a brand new car with that new car smell, and watch out! We hear it. Again, depending on the product, hearing can be a clincher. Just think about the sound of the surround sound connected to that TV. Cool! We taste it. Some have a really hard time letting a hot fudge and warm brownie sundae go by; it just tastes too good!

You're probably wondering what advertising has to do with our spiritual lives. Again, people don't buy in to God's love until they experience it. They're more likely to buy in to God's love when they connect to it. They need to see it. They do so by observing how we live and what we do. They need to touch it. The comfort of a loving hand expresses compassion for hurting people. They need to hear it. Listening to someone tell them how important they are to God can move someone from feeling empty to feeling they are of great worth. They need to taste it. Someone who is hungry experiences the love of God when those who love provide a warm meal that meets a need. They need to smell it. Taking care of someone's physical needs by providing a warm shower for a person who is filthy proves a concern for the well being of others.

We can show love in many ways. We need to be involved in helping people discover that God's love exists.
Q: What have you been doing with your life that proves you are motivated to show God's love?

Living in the present

"For you have spent enough time in the past doing what pagans choose to do—living in debauchery, lust, drunkenness, orgies, carousing and detestable idolatry" (1 Peter 4:3). We know the three dimensions of time: past, present, and future. So often believers go backwards in time, back to the past, and behave in ways that once revealed a motivation that didn't honor God. Those who go back to the past begin to live like pagans, involving themselves in actions that don't put God on display. In fact, these actions keep people from seeing who God really is. The way some believers live in the present makes a difference for the future, but it's a negative difference.

The believer who reverts back to an unhealthy lifestyle gives weight to the claim of many who don't give their lives to God. They may say something like this: "I see no reason to give my life to God, because those who claim to know Him are just like me. I see no difference. They're hypocrites." Have you heard anything like that statement before? The truth is that believers can all be hypocritical. We all have lapses and revert to the past. We should never make it seem that we're perfect or that we won't make mistakes. We need to be honest with people about our flaws. However, the more we revert to a previous lifestyle, the more difficult coming to know God will be for those who don't know Him. We don't need to go backwards.

Believers can go backwards because they've had a turning point. Nonbelievers have never gone forward by making a decision to live with a new motivation and attitude. Believers have had what I call a service turning point. We once served ourselves, but we turned to God to serve Him. The Scriptures call this repentance. Check out the Scripture. "First to those in Damascus, then to those in Jerusalem and in all Judea, and to the Gentiles also, I preached that they should repent and turn to God and prove their repentance by their deeds" (Acts 26:20). Our deeds are our service, the key to our positive

the fully devoted life

impact. We should serve in the present: **today**! We reach out and meet needs that keep people from seeing God. But first, we notice needs. Let's do an exercise to help us identify the needs of those in our circles of influence.

We filled out a circle of influence in chapter three which helped us identify people who don't know God. What are their needs? Write their names below, and describe their struggles.

Q: What needs do non-believers who are in my family have?

Q: What needs do my non-believing friends have?

Q: What needs do my non-believing neighbors have?

Q: What needs do my non-believing classmates have?

Q: What needs do those I casually know (acquaintances) have?

Q: What needs do the people in my traffic patterns have?

Being strong under pressure

"They think it strange that you do not plunge with them into the same flood of dissipation, and they heap abuse on you" (1 Peter 4:4). People who live the self-serving lifestyle want others to do the same thing. Self-serving people put pressure on others to join them. Many pressure others in order to feel better about their own behavior. If they can get you to become like them, not only do they feel better, but they stop you from sharing the message that needs to be heard. Remember that they haven't truly come to understand who God is and what He's about. They need us to be strong and not to compromise so that God's message comes through loud and clear.

Q: If people have been leading you away from God, what pressures have they been putting on you?

People can have one of two views.

- They believe that life is about investing in self, which will result in happiness. They live to please themselves. This belief is false.
- They believe that life is about investing in others, which brings joy. They live to please God. This belief is true.

When people put pressure on us, we need to identify which of these two views they believe.

Serving for change

"For this is the reason the gospel was preached even to those who are now dead, so that they might be judged according to men in regard to the body, but live according to God in regard to the spirit" (1 Peter 4:6). We always honor the one to whom we're committed. Commitment comes from the heart. The heart is where our spirit comes in. The spirit that motivates us drives our service, whether for self or others. We live to please the spirit that's in control. We are to follow God's Spirit. A difference exists between God's Spirit and the spirit of this world. Check out the difference.

- God's Spirit leads us to invest, not to take.
- God's Spirit builds and doesn't destroy.
- God's Spirit inspires and doesn't discourage.
- God's Spirit moves us forward to improve the world, not backwards to destroy it.

We need to identify which spirit is the motivating force of those we know. People in our circle who follow the wrong spirit need our service. What about the spirit that controls you? Answer the questions.

Q: Which spirit do your actions show is in control?

Q: What are you doing to make sure that God's Spirit is in control?

Having a clear mind

"The end of all things is near. Therefore be clear minded and self-controlled so that you can pray" (1 Peter 4:7). We have one of two minds. The clear mind thinks without obstruction and can see things as they really are. The clouded mind is polluted and distorts reality. We must see people and situations clearly. We must understand why they are who they are and why they do what they do. We often take the actions of others personally and become angry. This anger leads to bitterness, which leads to aggressive behavior, whether passive or forceful. We become so angry when we focus on what people do instead of why they do so. As long as anger clouds our minds, we won't work to make the proper impact. Remember that unhealthy behavior comes from an inward disease. Instead of getting mad at the behavior, treat that disease. Only one medicine cures the disease of sin: love.

Q: How do the actions of others affect how you see them?

Q: If you've become angry or bitter because of what others have done to you, what can you do to change your attitude?

Being self-controlled

"The end of all things is near. Therefore be clear minded and self-controlled so that you can pray" (1 Peter 4:7). Now we see the other part of the verse. We need to be self-controlled. The Scripture tells us why; we are self-controlled so that we can pray. Our speaking to God is a major part of our service to others. In fact, our service should begin with prayer. We need to hear from God so that we can know what to do. So what's the big deal about self-control? The deal is that pure prayer has power! Those who pray with a clear mind and a pure heart pray with the right motives. We pray for the right reason. We want others to succeed. We want God to use us to encourage others to know the good life.

Q: Are you controlled by your circumstances, or are you in control as you face them? Why?

Q: How has your reaction to events affected your prayer life?

Having a deep love

"Above all, love each other deeply, because love covers over a multitude of sins" (1 Peter 4:8). I forgive when I love others more than myself. The Scripture says that love covers a multitude of sins. In other words, our forgiveness no longer holds evil actions against those who did them. I can't hold their behavior against them if I'm going to serve them. Love overcomes the pain we feel as the result of someone's sin and changes the way we respond to those we forgive.

Have a deep and powerful love that overcomes the hatred of this world. This love prepares us to reach out even to the worst of those who live around us. When I love others above all else, I:

- Notice them = I give them my attention.
- See their need = I see what stresses they face.
- Long for their need to be met = I want the best for them.
- Forgive them = I don't hold what they've done to harm me against them.
- Take action = I do what I can to meet their needs for their success.

We often ignore people who hurt us. Their behavior has a tendency to affect the love we have for them. If they treat us well, we love them more, and if they treat us poorly, we love them less. We need to remember God's approach. His love for us isn't dependent upon our behavior. He wants to change our behavior, and He knows that love is the cure. We must give others our attention. An indication of our fluctuating love is the attention we give. If we avoid people, we may avoid them because our love has diminished. We need to learn to look beyond their actions. When we do, we're able to see their stress - the pressure that causes their behavior.

Q: How has your love for others affected your service to them? Maybe your love is shallow and not deep. If so, keep this condition in mind as you answer the question.

Speaking correctly for God

"If anyone speaks, he should do it as one speaking the very words of God" (1 Peter 4:11). My words should communicate the following message:

- "You matter."
- "You're worthwhile."
- "I want the best for you."

We just learned about the power of love. As God believes we're worthwhile, we need to see others as being worthwhile. Our effort communicates how we really feel about who they are. If we represent God, we communicate the same message that He gives to us.

Q: What message do you communicate to people about their worth?

Q: Is this message consistent with how God feels about you?

Serving with strength

"If anyone serves, he should do it with the strength God provides, so that in all things God may be praised through Jesus Christ. To him be the glory and the power for ever and ever. Amen" (1 Peter 4:11). We can't control how others will receive our service, but we can control how and to what extent we serve. Sometimes others meet our service with harmful rejection. We feel attacked. Our strength shouldn't depend upon people's opinion of us but on our belief in the message we deliver. If we believe that message, then rejection won't weaken us; it will burden us for the one who's missing out on the good life.

Q: How do you respond to those who lash out against your message?

Q: Is God pleased with this response?

God, I know that You have created me on purpose for a purpose. I thank You for wanting me on Your team. I ask that You help me as I discover who You've created me to be. I want to serve You.

Chapter Seven
The Work:
Imagine a life that engages the community.

For we are God's workmanship, created in Christ Jesus to do good works, which God prepared in advance for us to do.

Ephesians 2:10

Terry Lane knows what it means to make a difference. This Jacksonville, Florida businessman became convicted about the neighborhood where his business was located. Because of the success of his cabinet making company, he moved to a larger facility on the northwest side of town. Little did he know that his new neighborhood had one of the highest crime rates in the city. One particular problem area was a housing complex adjacent to Lane's facility. He became keenly aware of his new neighbors when the police began calling nightly after responding to the facility's break-in alarm. One officer told him that the housing complex was known as "The Rock." He explained that the complex got the name because dealers sold more crack cocaine there than anywhere else in Jacksonville.

Terry didn't allow this information to discourage him. He believed that God was calling him to reach out to the neighborhood kids. He did so by buying some basketballs and throwing them over the fence. He wasn't about to take his life into his own hands by setting foot on the property. His gift must have worked. One day, some kids playing under a tractor trailer saw him, yelled, "There's the man," and began to run. Lane called to them and asked if they wanted something to drink. He took them inside, and the relationship began. When the next Monday afternoon came, Lane noticed some noise out in the reception area. He came around the corner to find sixteen kids. When the receptionist asked them if she could help them, they asked, "Where's the big man with the beard?" They wanted the guy who had the key to the soda machine. These kids connected with Lane, and before he knew it, he had thirty-five kids coming over after school. Many of them had parents who were drug addicts. Some came over hungry. Some were undisciplined and needed guidance.

Ten years after the relationship began with the kids, he sold his shares in the company and started Metro Inner City Sunday School. What happened over those years is amazing. When the kids got older, they started programs for students in the area. The love was spreading. Terry asked the owner of the apartment complex if he could have an apartment. The owner agreed, and within five years Lane established a community center there called Metro Kids Konnection. The staff there feed over one hundred forty-five children, not only with food for their physical condition, but also with instruction academically and with love spiritually.[11] Why did all of this outreach happen? All of this good came because a man had a vision to change a community through some kids who needed Christ. He lived his life to accomplish a great purpose.

God created me on purpose for a purpose.

Who?

Who created me? God created me; I am His handiwork. He created me for a task. I mentioned earlier that I ride motorcycles. Riding is a great release for me. I'm also a big fan of shows on television about motorcycle building. Seeing what goes into making some of the most innovative bikes in the world amazes me. I'm struck by how the mechanics always begin. They have a vision of what they're creating. They never start without having what they're building in mind. Not only do they build it to look cool, but they also build it to function. After all, a bike that can't go from point A to point B isn't very useful.

God had a vision of us before he made us. He created us with purpose. We read about this purpose above in Ephesians 2:10. He prepared us in advance to function and to accomplish what He's called us to do. That's who we are.

How?

Think about a car. Every part is important, but one is critical: the motor. Without it, it goes nowhere. The motor is the power source. Our most important spiritual part is our power source: the heart. The heart is the motivating source of life, and should be motivated to look like Christ. God begins there. If we have the wrong motivation, we won't accomplish our purpose.

A transformation takes place when Christ becomes a part of us. We've already learned about transformation, but it's important to consider again. The word *transform* means "to take something that is in one condition and change it into another." In our case, God transformed something dead into something alive. We transform when God transforms our bad motor (our heart) and gives us new life. Christ is the source of our new life. If we rely on Him for our power, the other parts of life begin to reveal Him. If we don't, they don't!

Why?

This question leads us to why we were created. We know we were created on purpose, but what is that purpose? God created us to do good works. Let's define the types of work.

- **Good work**: activity that influences something to function correctly. Someone did the work to help us recognize our spiritual need. Those who helped us recognize this performed good work. We do good work when we help those who are spiritually dysfunctional begin to function

correctly. We're like good mechanics who actually fix what's broken.
- **Bad work**: activity that influences something to function incorrectly. Those who do bad work encourage others to live a spiritually dysfunctional life. They don't influence them toward Christ; they encourage them to love themselves and to disregard others. We're like bad mechanics who don't fix what's broken; we make things worse.

Q: What kind of work have you most often been performing? How have you been doing this work?

What?

What's next? I need to do the good work! Here's the cool thing about that work. He prepared the work for us to do in advance. He knew what He needed us to do, and He created a "part" to fulfill that function. You're the carburetor! Okay, maybe you're the handlebars. Whatever you are, you're important because He created the job for you, not for someone else. He did it for you!

When?

When do I do this work? Now may be a good time! We weren't created to sit; we were created to serve! God didn't create a part to put on the shelf; He created a part to put in the body. In fact, God doesn't put us on the shelf; He puts us in the body. Here's the problem: some parts don't work.

There are times that the parts of the body of Christ, the church, don't work. We've joined the other parts, but we don't do what we were meant to do. What's the problem? We have a connection problem. The power source for each of us (each part) is Christ. If we don't allow His love to rule us with a love that leads us to notice the needs of others and long to help, then we don't work.

If we're not doing our part, we've allowed our desires to shift away from living like Christ to living for ourselves. This shift is a big deal. If we don't work, God doesn't throw us out of the body and replace us. He created the job for us, not for someone else. So what does He do to correct the problem? He keeps doing things in our lives to encourage us to change our motivation by changing our power source. He does so in an effort to bring our service back to life.

God is preparing me.

Let's look at another passage of Scripture and learn some important lessons.

> It was he who gave some to be apostles, some to be prophets, some to be evangelists, and some to be pastors and teachers, to prepare God's people for works of service, so that the body of Christ may be built up until we all reach unity in the faith and in the knowledge of the Son of God and become mature, attaining to the whole measure of the fullness of Christ. Then we will no longer be infants, tossed back and forth by the waves, and blown here and there by every wind of teaching and by the cunning and craftiness of men in their deceitful scheming. Instead, speaking the truth in love, we will in all things grow up into him who is the Head, that is, Christ. From him the whole body, joined and held together by every supporting ligament, grows and builds itself up in love, as each part does its work.
>
> Ephesians 4:11-16

God uses people to prepare us. Here's something awesome about God. He doesn't give us a job without helping us understand its importance and how to do it. God has placed people in positions to assist us as we learn to serve and as we serve. The Scriptures teach us about those who are to train us.

The Examples, also known as apostles, were those who followed Jesus and performed tasks of ministry. Jesus sent them out into the towns and villages to meet the needs of people. As a leader, one of the best pieces of advice I've ever received was from my dad. He told me, "Tim, don't ever ask anyone to do anything you're not willing to do yourself. You have to lead by example." The apostle sets the example by working with others to achieve the goal.

The Visionaries, also known as prophets, can see the future. They aren't fortune tellers; they are future tellers. They clearly view what God is calling us to do. People need to know what they're trying to accomplish before they do their work. If they don't, they have no sense of value or meaning in what they do. If they're sold out to achieving what they've been shown, they'll do the work with great enthusiasm. People need to know their work matters and that it's for a great cause. The visionary motivates us to get involved and stay involved.

The Directors of Marketing are also known as evangelists. We learned that all of us are Marketing Supervisors earlier in the book. All of us manage our lives in a way that helps others see their need for what we have. All of us share our faith openly with others. An evangelist has a special calling and ability to help people see their need for Christ. They keep the importance of our sharing our story in front of us, not letting us forget the importance of our message. They encourage us to share Good News!

The Shepherd, also known as the pastor, is there to meet needs, providing an example of what it means to serve the hurting inside and outside of the church. He feeds the flock by sharing the truths of God's Word, encouraging others to grow into fully devoted followers of Christ.

The Trainer is also known as the teacher. We need someone to teach us how to perform our tasks. The trainer provides instruction on what we are to do and why we are to do it. They also hold us accountable to fulfilling our roles of service and our continual movement toward becoming mature followers of Christ.

Q: Who does God use to prepare you for service? If no one helps you, who do you need to help you prepare for service?

Q: What are your teachers doing to get you ready?

God has a purpose for my work.

Reggie McNeal tells this story. "I was sitting on a bench on a beach boardwalk late one afternoon, resting after an hour walk. I had passed a woman in a green uniform pushing a broom several times. She came toward my bench doing her meticulous sweeping of the sidewalk. Suddenly she stopped, wiped her forehead, and rested on her broom. I called out to her: 'You do a great job.' 'Thank you,' she replied. Then she added something that explained why the sidewalk behind her was spotless. 'I just believe people want to walk on a clean sidewalk.'" He reflected on what happened and wrote, "I was humbled to be in the presence of a worker who viewed her task with such significance. Whatever the park service was paying her, there's no way they could have demanded the excellence she brought to her work. That kind of motivation comes from within.[12] Knowing that our work matters, matters!

We just learned that a visionary helps people see what they're working for. Knowing why we're serving and what we're accomplishing is important for us. The church functions as a team, and each team member needs to know his role in the movement toward the goal God has set. Some key phrases appear in Ephesians 4:12-13. Let's take a look at them again. "To prepare God's people for works of service, so that the body of Christ may be built up until we all reach unity in the faith and in the knowledge of the Son of God and become mature, attaining to the whole measure of the fullness of Christ" (Ephesians 4:12-13). From this Scripture, we see why we do the work that we are called to perform. We've already seen that God has called some people to help us accomplish our tasks.

My purpose is to lead the lost to Christ.

We accomplish our tasks together as a team. Paul wrote that we are trained so that "the body of Christ may be built up until we all reach unity in the faith and in the knowledge of the Son of God" (Ephesians 4:12-13). Circle the word *all* in the Scripture. Paul teaches that we should do what we do until everyone has been unified through faith in Jesus Christ. We all need to have knowledge of the Son of God. And so we don't stop serving until every human being knows Christ as their Savior. God's goal is for everyone to know Jesus. His goal is my purpose.

Q: When you serve, do you do it to feel good or to help people see their need for Jesus?

My purpose is to become mature and to lead others.

God wants everyone on the team to be mature. Paul wrote that we are to "become mature, attaining to the whole measure of the fullness of Christ." Isn't that verse what this book is about? It's our theme passage. God wants us to be fully devoted followers of Christ. He defines what maturity is. Maturity is being full. It's the whole measure. There is no room for any other power source because Christ controls every part of my life. Those who are full ooze love. Not only should I want that love for myself, but I should also want that love for others. We learned previously that we reach those who don't know Christ. Once they do, we help them as they move toward maturity. That help is a function of the church.

Q: Are you becoming more mature or less mature spiritually?

Q: Are you making better decisions or worse decisions about life?

Learning to live the "no longer" life

I must overcome seasickness.

Some love boating. They love to hear the water splash against the side of the boat and smell the sea water. Paul talked about the waves and the winds coming and tossing us back and forth. He uses this image to illustrate what happens when we are subjected to people who teach us false information. We rock and roll and get off course when we believe them. We're tossed about. Look again at what the Scripture teaches us: "Then we will no longer be infants,

the fully devoted life

tossed back and forth by the waves, and blown here and there by every wind of teaching and by the cunning and craftiness of men in their deceitful scheming" (Ephesians 4:14).

Our being blown about and out of control is a sure sign of our immaturity. We are "no longer" to live that way. I live the "no longer" life. I grow up in my faith enough to be able to withstand the pressures that come at me.

It really gets old, doesn't it? Being blown around spiritually is no fun at all. Although we do well for a while, something or someone comes along to distract us away from Christ, and we lose our full measure. Something else creeps in. We experience spiritual seasickness. We should want to face the temptations and **"no longer"** yield. God requires that resolve from us to serve and serve well. We must stay on course when the wind blows. If I'm going to live the **"no longer"** life, we need to live by a principle. We'll learn about it after answering these questions.

Q: Do you feel spiritually seasick? What temptations continue to affect you?

Q: What are you doing to overcome this weakness?

the fully devoted life

I must master the "instead principle."

Take a look at the description of what this principle is.

> The Instead Principle:
> *"Instead of including things that rock my life, I include things that stabilize my life."*

We get blown off course when we only subject ourselves to the things that blow us back and forth and blow us off course. We need to include stabilizers. We need stabilizers in the Christian life. We need to add things to our lives that combat the dangerous things that come against us. Not only do we need to pray and study God's Word, but we also need to add people in our lives who can hold us accountable. They are our stabilizers. We need people who notice when we're getting blown off course and direct us back to the lives we should be living. Instead of living the Christian life on our own, we include people who can help stabilize us.

Q: Are you trying to live the Christian life alone? Why?

Q: Stabilizers are people who hold us accountable. Who are your stabilizers?

Being a "supporter"

Being a supporting ligament

Once again, we learn an important lesson from Paul's letter to the church. He wrote: "From him the whole body, joined and held together by every supporting ligament, grows and builds itself up in love, as each part does its work" (Ephesians 4:16). We're held together by every supporting ligament. We're held together when we support one another, when we appreciate how God created others and know the importance of what they do for Him. We want our brothers and sisters to succeed. Our encouragement matters. Getting frustrated and quitting the team is easy for people. But when our team quits, we begin to lose the game, which is not cool.

We need to be cheerleaders. We're to serve not only the lost in hopes that they'll come to God but also fellow believers who are burdened. All of us need the encouragement that comes from love. Love is the ligament, the glue that binds us together, keeping our focus on the goal of reaching out to the hurting.

Q: What do you do to encourage others on the team to stay in the game?

Q: What could you do to become more supportive?

Supporting body building

We've learned that the body of Christ is the church. We do work that strengthens the church. We do those things that improve the image of the church. We do things that cause people to see the church in a positive way.

We also remove things from our lives that cause people to see Christ in a negative way. Here is some advice. Don't wear a Christian T-shirt while you're looking at videos in the store that you have no business seeing. Here's a suggestion. Just don't look at the videos. How about more advice? Don't put a Jesus sticker on your car if you frequently speed, experience road rage, or like cutting people off. These might be lighthearted examples, but people associate the church with what people in the church do.

Q: What do you need to remove from your life that gives a bad impression of the church?

Knowing what I'm called to do

Do you know what God wants you to do? How do we know what we're called to do? Here is a statement that can guide us:

"If you see the need, and know that God has given you the ability to meet that need, and are passionate about meeting the need, then that constitutes a call."

That statement closely connects with one from Frederick Buechner, an American writer and preacher, taught years ago. He wrote, "The place God calls you to is the place where your deep gladness and the world's deep hunger meet."[13]

Three pieces fit together to complete the picture of what God wants.

- Need
- Ability
- Passion

Answer the questions below as you begin to think of what God has for you to do.

Q: What needs do you see?

Q: Has God given you the ability to meet those needs?

Q: Are you passionate enough to learn how better to meet those needs?

Q: When will you start?

A part of having the ability to meet needs involves knowing what we are gifted to do. God has given us all spiritual gifts which he expects us to use for Him. This concept gets us back to what Paul said. Check it out again. "For it is by grace you have been saved, through faith—and this not from yourselves, it is the gift of God—not by works, so that no one can boast. For we are God's workmanship, created in Christ Jesus to do good works, which God prepared in advance for us to do" (Ephesians 2:8-10).

If He's prepared us in advance, then He's created us with what we need to do His work. Below is a resource to help you in the discovery process as you determine the gifts God has given you. Take some time and follow the instructions to complete The Discovery Test.

THE DISCOVERY TEST
Understanding My Gifts and Talents

Place a score below each statement which best describes you: 0 = doesn't describe me at all and 10 = perfectly describes me. After writing your scores, total them and place this number in the space provided.[14]

Administration
- I'm an organizer.
Score: _____
- I love details.
Score: _____
- I love developing plans to accomplish goals.
Score: _____
- I love to help others who are weak in organization.
Score: _____
- I am able to see events before they occur.
Score: _____

    Total Score: _____

Craftsmanship
- I'm a handyman/handywoman.
Score: _____
- I love working with building tools.
Score: _____
- I understand how objects come together and work.
Score: _____
- I love working with my hands.
Score: _____
- I love to design things that help others accomplish their tasks.
Score: _____

    Total Score: _____

Creative Communication
- I love teaching creatively through the arts.
Score: _____
- I love to participate in music, art, drama, etc.
Score: _____
- I love trying new things.
Score: _____
- I love to use my imagination.
Score: _____
- I enjoy working with others to accomplish creative ideas.
Score: _____

   Total Score: _____

Discernment
- I'm good at determining if people are being honest.
Score: _____
- I'm good at determining people's motives.
Score: _____
- I quickly can determine what is right and wrong in a situation.
Score: _____
- I can easily determine if someone is teaching the truth.
Score: _____
- I have a clear understanding of what is occurring in various situations.
Score: _____

   Total Score: _____

Encouragement
- I love to build people up.

Score: _____
- I love to help people reach their full potential.

Score: _____
- I enjoy sharing the truths of God's Word with those who need direction.

Score: _____
- I enjoy helping people mature in their faith.

Score: _____
- I am honest with people when they have failures.

Score: _____

   Total Score: _____

Evangelism
- I love telling people the good news of Christ.

Score: _____
- I build relationships, wanting others to discover Christ.

Score: _____
- I communicate Christ with others in an understandable way.

Score: _____
- I am open about my faith.

Score: _____
- Daily, I am aware of those around me and long for them to know Christ.

Score: _____

   Total Score: _____

Faith
- I believe God will answer my prayers.

Score: _____
- I am not overcome by difficult circumstances.

Score: _____
- I believe that God has a great purpose for my life.

Score: _____
- I encourage others to trust in God.

Score: _____
- My decisions are not based on the opinion of man; they are based on God's direction.

Score: _____

    Total Score: _____

Giving
- I love to give my resources to help people in need.

Score: _____
- I give over and above my tithe to invest in God's kingdom.

Score: _____
- Money does not control me.

Score: _____
- I manage my money in order to give to God first.

Score: _____
- I believe that everything I have are resources provided by God and are under my care.

Score: _____

    Total Score: _____

Helps
- I'm a "behind the scenes" person.

Score: _____
- I love to come alongside people and help them accomplish their tasks.

Score: _____
- No job is beneath me.

Score: _____
- I consistently look for ways to help others.

Score: _____
- I'm willing to learn how to do new tasks to be helpful to others.

Score: _____

    Total Score: _____

Intercession
- I love to pray for others.

Score: _____
- My prayer life is not limited by time.

Score: _____
- I believe that God will answer my prayers.

Score: _____
- When I see people in need, I desire to lift them up in prayer.

Score: _____
- I am excited when people ask me to pray.

Score: _____

    Total Score: _____

Leadership
- I love to motivate people.

Score: _____
- I am able to visualize the future and communicate it with others.

Score: _____
- I set goals to accomplish vision.

Score: _____
- I hold people accountable to their tasks.

Score: _____
- I am able to motivate people to join me in the journey to accomplish vision.

Score: _____

    Total Score: _____

Mercy
- I feel the pain of those who are hurting and long to help them.

Score: _____
- I enjoy helping people as they go through difficult circumstances.

Score: _____
- I enjoy helping people no matter what others think of them.

Score: _____
- I see people as someone created and loved by God.

Score: _____
- I help others see the positive, knowing God is in control.

Score: _____

    Total Score: _____

Preaching
- I enjoy speaking in public.

Score: _____
- I speak truth without compromise.

Score: _____
- I help people see the difference between living for God and living for self.

Score: _____
- I have a clear understanding of what is right and wrong within our culture.

Score: _____
- I love to share the truth of God's Word with others.

Score: _____

    Total Score: _____

Teaching
- I help people learn God's Word through communicating in understandable ways.

Score: _____
- I enjoy studying God's Word in preparation to share truth with others.

Score: _____
- I enjoy reading the insights of others who give explanation of God's Word.

Score: _____
- I communicate God's Word that encourages life change.

Score: _____
- I enjoy helping others become more like Christ.

Score: _____

    Total Score: _____

Wisdom
- I have a clear understanding of God's will.

Score: _____
- I can determine solutions to problems that are presented.

Score: _____
- I am able to listen to opinions and to determine the best course of action.

Score: _____
- I envision the future and understand and am realistic about what may happen.

Score: _____
- I have understanding about situations that others do not have.

Score: _____

Total Score: _____

According to your scores (the three highest), what three gifts best describe you?

_____

_____

_____

Now that you've completed the test, go back to the answers you provided to the questions just prior to the test. Remember, our call involves need, ability, and passion. You've identified different needs that you see. Do the gifts you've just discovered about yourself match those needs? Although these factors may match, you may not have a true passion for meeting that need. Which of these needs do you have a passion to meet? Guess what! You've just discovered your call.

Remember, passion and action go together. Your passion for that ministry should motivate you to get involved in meeting the needs you've identified. Answer the following questions.

Q: Who do you need to talk to in order to get started?

Q: What do you need to do to prepare yourself to serve?

Q: When will you start?

Let's think back about something else we learned. God didn't create you to sit on the shelf. He's already placed you in the body, the church. Are you working? Are you accomplishing your role? It's time to get involved and make a difference.

God, thank You for insight into who I am. You have created me to impact the world, and I give myself to You to be used for this purpose. I ask You to reveal Your calling for my life. Please open my eyes to the needs of those around me who can benefit from who You've created me to be.

the fully devoted life

Section Five
Treasures:
The Resources to Share

Chapter Eight
The Giver:
Imagine a life that invests in eternity.

"I the LORD do not change. So you, O descendants of Jacob, are not destroyed. Ever since the time of your forefathers you have turned away from my decrees and have not kept them. Return to me, and I will return to you," says the LORD Almighty. "But you ask, 'How are we to return?' Will a man rob God? Yet you rob me. But you ask, 'How do we rob you?' In tithes and offerings. You are under a curse—the whole nation of you—because you are robbing me. Bring the whole tithe into the storehouse, that there may be food in my house. Test me in this," says the LORD Almighty, "and see if I will not throw open the floodgates of heaven and pour out so much blessing that you will not have room enough for it. I will prevent pests from devouring your crops, and the vines in your fields will not cast their fruit," says the LORD Almighty. "Then all the nations will call you blessed, for yours will be a delightful land," says the LORD Almighty. "You have said harsh things against me," says the LORD. "Yet you ask, 'What have we said against you?' You have said, 'It is futile to serve God. What did we gain by carrying out his requirements and going about like mourners before the LORD Almighty? But now we call the arrogant blessed. Certainly the evildoers prosper, and even those who challenge God escape.'" Then those who feared the LORD talked with each other, and the LORD listened and heard. A scroll of remembrance was written in his presence concerning those who feared the LORD and honored his name. "They will be mine," says the LORD Almighty, "in the day when I make up my treasured possession. I will spare them, just as in compassion a man spares his son who serves him. And you will again see the distinction between the righteous and the wicked, between those who serve God and those who do not."

Malachi 3:6-18

Our being fully devoted followers of Christ also involves our managing the resources He has placed under our care in an obedient and wise way. We are to do this in order to make investments that matter. Do you feel good about what you give as an investment in God's kingdom? Giving tends to be one of the last disciplines that believers master because it requires change in the way we approach our resources and finances. We need to learn what God has to say about our obedient giving. We'll begin by learning that we need to treat with respect and care what God has given us to manage for Him.

Avoiding wrong financial activity

Scripture gets to the point when it deals with those who aren't faithful in giving. The Bible goes so far as to say that we rob God. When people steal our stuff, we obviously don't feel good. We feel violated. For God to say that we're robbing Him is a pretty big deal. That statement gives us a view of how He sees our behavior.

In our world today, we may even be able to use another word: embezzlement. We become embezzlers when we take money from God and put it somewhere else that benefits us. Embezzlers of our day do something similar. They are entrusted with someone's money, but they begin taking it to use for their own personal benefit. These sneak thieves put the funds in a place where they believe they'll be protected from prosecution. Into the foreign bank account goes Grandma's IRA.

This example is very similar to what we do with God. He entrusted us with His resources, and we take them and move them from His bank account to ours. We put God's funds into a foreign bank account. We make that money our own instead of managing what He's given us for Him. We take possession of God's possessions. This action doesn't sit well with Him, and it shouldn't sit well with us. For many, it doesn't, but they don't do anything to correct their financial practices. We should strive to become obedient and to feel the joy of managing what is His in a way that brings change to our community and world.

Q: How do you think God feels about those who take what He's given to use for their own kingdom?

Q: If you were God, how would you respond?

Knowing God's financial expectations

"Bring the whole tithe into the storehouse, that there may be food in my house. Test me in this," says the LORD Almighty, "and see if I will not throw open the floodgates of heaven and pour out so much blessing that you will not have room enough for it" (Malachi 3:10). We're to be "whole givers." We're to give the whole tithe. Why? Why should we give a whole tithe? God instructed us to do so.

We know that God has good reasons for His commands, but our enthusiasm level grows when we know what those reasons are. We enthusiastically give when we're excited about who receives our gifts. To know that people will be changed for the better because of our investment causes the excitement level to rise. Nothing is better than seeing people rescued because we've been obedient to God in our giving. So why give the whole tithe? If we don't, we limit what can be done through giving.

The founders of Empty Tomb, Inc. conducted research to track Christian giving behaviors as well as global needs. Researchers estimated that $70-$80 billion a year could meet the necessary human needs of those who suffer in poverty around the globe. The researchers state: "That figure of $70-$80 billion may sound like anything but good news. God may be generous, you may agree, but has he been that generous? Consider this: If church members in the United States would increase their giving to 10 percent of their income, there could be an additional $86 billion available for overseas missions."[15]

Many Christians debate the amount we should give in tithe. Some see the tithe as an indefinable amount, while others use the literal meaning of the word to mean one-tenth of income. The Bible uses the word *tithe* several times to represent one-tenth. Some may use the passage that Paul wrote to the church in Corinth. Let's take a look at it again. "Each man should give what he has decided in his heart to give, not reluctantly or under compulsion, for God loves a cheerful giver" (2 Corinthians 9:7).

Paul used the phrase "each man should give what he has decided in his heart to give." Some who argue against giving one-tenth use this verse to say that the tithing percentage is a personal choice. They say that we give what's in our hearts, which might be different for me than for you. For me, tithe might be two percent, and for you it may be ten. What's the answer? Let's think about one of the reasons why Paul may have given the instruction. We give what we've decided in our hearts because God doesn't want us to give with the wrong attitude. He wants us to give cheerfully, not reluctantly or out of coercion. Giving bitterly does us no good. There's more to this.

God wouldn't have given us a command to do something He didn't expect us to do; He just wants us to be cheerful while we do so. He wants us to obey Him because we want to obey, not because we have to obey. God does want us to give the whole tithe (ten percent); He just wants us to give with the right heart. God has two goals for us:

- To have hearts that want to obey fully in giving our tithe.
- To live lives that work toward obeying fully in giving our tithe.

If you don't have a heart that wants to obey fully in giving, chances are you won't make any changes in your life to obey fully. The solution to overcoming this problem is to change the motivation of our hearts. We aren't to be motivated to give out of obligation, we are to be motivated to give out of desire. We develop desire when we know the difference our giving can make for those who are hurting. Our desire grows when we want others to see God's love. Remember, we are fully devoted followers of Christ when we obey God in everything. This includes our giving. Let me state this in another way. We aren't fully devoted followers of Christ if we aren't obedient in managing His resources in a way that pleases Him. If we are passionate about God, we'll want to obey. If our hearts are right, we go to work making sure we are on a path that meets God's expectations. God plans that we cheerfully increase our giving until we obey Him completely.

Knowing what type of giver I am

Some are obedient, and others are not. If our hearts are right, we work to get on the right track. Before we do so, we need to know what kind of giver we are. We see four types of givers. Check them out.

The "non-givers:" They don't give anything. They can't have cheerful hearts because they don't make any investment. They know they should, but they don't. They know that they receive ministry which has a financial cost (using facilities to worship, etc.), and they know that they can enjoy the ministry because other people give. Most likely, they feel convicted about not giving. Perhaps they even want to give, but they feel they can't.

The "partial givers:" Most people give something. Research tells us that the vast majority of Americans give to philanthropic organizations, whether the church or other social organizations. A 2006 study revealed that Americans who give to charities outnumber those who vote. As of 2006, Americans gave more than $200 billion a year.[16] Many who attend church do give; however, they haven't reached the point of obedient giving. They give what is in their hearts, cheerfully, but they do not give a tithe. Many in this group want to give their tithe fully, but they don't feel that they are able.

The "whole givers:" They bring the whole tithe into the storehouse. They completely obey God by giving cheerfully and with great joy because they know they're living up to God's expectations. The more money they make, the more they give to impact a world that needs Christ. And the more they give, the happier they are.

James Kennedy told a story about a wealthy man who didn't believe he could tithe anymore. He came to the former chaplain of the U.S. Senate, Peter Marshall, and asked for his advice. He said, "I have a problem. I've been tithing for some time. It wasn't too bad when I was making $20,000 a year. I could afford to give the $2,000. But you see, now I'm making $500,000, and there is just no way I can afford to give away $50,000 a year." Marshall thought about what he'd said but had no advice to offer him. Instead he said, "I think we ought to pray about it. Is that alright?" He agreed, so Dr. Marshall prayed - "Dear Lord, this man has a problem, and I pray that you will help him. Lord, reduce his salary back to the place where he can afford to tithe."[17] That prayer kind of puts things in perspective, doesn't it? I don't think his heart was quite right. What about you?

The "over givers:" An "over giver" gives over and above his tithe as an offering. He can do so out of monies that he sets aside above his tithe to invest in ministries that make a difference.

Some of you know of Patricia Heaton, who starred in *Everybody Loves Raymond*. Heaton, a strong believer, knows the importance of using money to change the world, and she's someone who has the resources to do so. Although she made a reported six million dollars per year from the TV show, she's more concerned about keeping things in perspective and teaching her children about a relationship with God. You can imagine how difficult this conviction must be on the Hollywood scene. She's open about her challenges, even with the way she sees money. She said, "I struggle to keep it simple. Obedience, sacrifice, and modesty are not real popular buzzwords out here. An issue I'm dealing with lately is, 'Do I have too much money, and am I being a good steward of it?' In fact, I was talking to a friend about tithing—just giving your 10 percent as opposed to giving until it actually starts costing you something, which is what I think tithing is all about."[18]

Some believers have the ability to give beyond a tithe to areas of need. This good practice reminds us about the importance of sacrifice. Those of wealth who give up things to benefit others remind themselves about the needs that are present in our world. They may give toward a mission endeavor, toward a student's way to camp, toward building facilities to make the church more effective in ministry, and the list goes on. Patricia Heaton was learning all about these opportunities.

Q: Are you a non giver, partial giver, whole giver, or over giver?

Q: If you are not a "whole giver," do you feel that it's important to be one? Why or why not?

Q: If you are a "non giver," what would it take for you to move up to a "partial giver?"

Q: If you are a "partial giver," what would it take for you to move up to a "whole giver?"

Q: If you are a "whole giver," what would it take for you to move up to an "over giver?"

Preparing for my financial future

What career do you want in the future? You may not know the answer to that question right now. Depending on your age, you may have plenty of time to decide. For some of you, the decision may need to be made soon. It's important to approach our occupation and the money that we earn in the right way. It may be that you don't have much money now, but that will change in the future as you begin working more regularly. We've learned about the types of givers and we want to make certain that we are the right type of giver – someone who is completely obedient to God in how we manage His resources.

We need to prepare for the future, so let's do some imagining! In the space below, write down an occupation that you are interested in.

_____.

We want to prepare ourselves to be financially obedient if we had a job in this field. How much do you think someone in this field makes annually? If you don't know, do some research and find out, or just make a guess. Write down that amount in the space below.

$_____.
(Annual Income)

Now that you know the annual amount, how much would that be on a monthly basis? Divide the annual salary by twelve and write down that number in the space below.

$_____.
(Monthly Income)

We'll be using this monthly amount to make a financial plan that honors God. You'll notice a budget on the following page that lists several items that you should consider when managing your income. We'll begin with giving to God's Kingdom. This is where you place the amount of your tithe. What is 10% of your monthly income? Write that number next to the "Giving to God" line item on your budget. The priority is to give to Him first. We do this to meet the needs of others. You also have needs and you're budget will reflect items that relate to them. When writing in amounts next to the budget items, use a number that represents what you really need. Often we think we need more than we do and it causes us to over spend, keeping us from investing in God's work.

Let's get started and complete the budget.

BUDGET
- Giving to God (tithe/gifts) _____
- Housing/Rent _____
- Savings _____
- Emergencies _____
- Health/Life Insurance _____
- Automobile Payment _____
- Automobile Insurance _____
- Automobile Maintenance (Repair/Oil) _____
- Gasoline _____
- Food/Home Products _____
- Clothing _____
- Electricity/Gas _____
- Water _____
- Telephone/Cable/Internet _____
- Garbage _____
- Home Maintenance _____
- Home Furnishings _____
- Medication _____
- Subscriptions (newspaper, etc.) _____
- Cleaning/Laundry _____
- Recreation/Vacation _____
- Gifts/Birthdays _____
- Miscellaneous _____
- Other[19] _____

TOTAL _____ _____

Is there money left over after paying your expenses? If so, we can use this money for "wants?" It's okay to have "wants" if we meet needs first, including our giving to God and meeting our basic needs. The money that is left over is called "available income." We know the amount by subtracting our total expenses from our income. Write the amount in the space below.

Available Income $_____
(Subtract expenses from income.)

You might be saying – "I don't have any available income." You might even say – "I don't have enough to pay my bills!" If that's the case, go back through the budget and make sure you budgeted for your "needs" and not "wants." If you don't begin learning how to budget this way now, it's very difficult to change as you enter the adult years. Make sure you seek God and ask Him to help you make good financial decisions that honor Him.

God, thank You for providing for my needs. You have called me to manage Your resources in a way that brings change in the hearts of the hurting. I ask You to help me as I use Your resources to impact others for You. Thank You for trusting me with Your possessions.

Chapter Nine
The Margin:
Imagine a life that conserves available resources.

Remember this: Whoever sows sparingly will also reap sparingly, and whoever sows generously will also reap generously. Each man should give what he has decided in his heart to give, not reluctantly or under compulsion, for God loves a cheerful giver. And God is able to make all grace abound to you, so that in all things at all times, having all that you need, you will abound in every good work. As it is written: "He has scattered abroad his gifts to the poor; his righteousness endures forever." Now he who supplies seed to the sower and bread for food will also supply and increase your store of seed and will enlarge the harvest of your righteousness. You will be made rich in every way so that you can be generous on every occasion, and through us your generosity will result in thanksgiving to God. This service that you perform is not only supplying the needs of God's people but is also overflowing in many expressions of thanks to God. Because of the service by which you have proved yourselves, men will praise God for the obedience that accompanies your confession of the gospel of Christ, and for your generosity in sharing with them and with everyone else. And in their prayers for you their hearts will go out to you, because of the surpassing grace God has given you. Thanks be to God for his indescribable gift!

2 Corinthians 9:6-15

How would you respond to the following statements? Next to "agree" or "disagree" place a check mark to represent what you believe.

- God wants people to be financially prosperous:
  __ agreed;   __ disagreed.
- Material wealth is a sign of God's blessing:
  __ agreed;   __ disagreed.
- Poverty can be a blessing from God:
  __ agreed;   __ disagreed.
- Jesus was not rich, and we should follow his example:
  __ agreed;   __ disagreed.
- If you give away your money to God, He will bless you with more money:
  __ agreed; __ disagreed.
- Christians in the U.S. don't do enough for the poor:
  __ agreed; __ disagreed
- Giving away 10 percent of your income is the minimum God expects:
  __ agreed; __ disagreed.

We have many different ideas about how finances relate to our faith. Having the right understanding of God's expectations concerning our giving is important for us. Let's spend some time learning some important lessons from God's Word.

Knowing that my giving results in getting

"Remember this: Whoever sows sparingly will also reap sparingly, and whoever sows generously will also reap generously" (2 Corinthians 9:6). We learned in the last chapter that knowing what we're giving to is great. It motivates us. The statement "knowing that my giving results in getting," sounds like a really selfish statement, but it's not. Think about the financial investments we make today. We have many choices. We can decide to start a new business, purchase real estate, or buy stocks or bonds, to name a few. Most of us want something called a yield from our financial choices. In other words, we want to earn money from our investments. The more the yield we earn, the better we consider the investment. Makes sense, right?

Think about our investments spiritually. The same is true. We use the money we have and expect something in return. Paul called our investment "sowing." The more we sow, the more we reap. You may have heard this very true statement put another way: "we reap what we sow." In this case, we don't give so we can get; we give so that others can get. The yield of the investment isn't our becoming financially wealthy; the yield is others becoming spiritually rich. Our hearts should desire this yield.

Having the right passion

> Each man should give what he has decided in his heart to give, not reluctantly or under compulsion, for God loves a cheerful giver. (2 Corinthians 9:7)

We give what we decide in our hearts to give.

We've learned that the passion of our hearts leads to the action we perform. This rule is true of our giving action. Let me restate this idea. The passions of our hearts lead to our giving actions. We give to the object of our passion. Passion is all about the heart. The way we spend our resources tells us a lot about the commitment of our hearts.

Q: What does your spending say about your passion?

We give in the right way.

This concept is not new to us. In the previous chapter, we learned that we are to be cheerful givers. This standard is not the only option we have. Take a look at three ways we can give. Two are the wrong way, and one is right. Wrong and right are all about attitude. "Each man should give what he has decided in his heart to give, not reluctantly or under compulsion, for God loves a cheerful giver" (2 Corinthians 9:7).

- **The Wrong Way**: Reluctantly. We learned that we give what we've decided in our hearts to give. God loves for us to be excited about the investments we make. Giving with a bad attitude does us no good. We aren't pleased, and we don't please God. He wants us to get to the point of obedient giving and to give with a happy heart. We give reluctantly when we're more concerned about investing in ourselves than in others. Our attention is on what we are giving up instead of what we are giving to. Those who are reluctant want to keep, not share.
- **Another Wrong Way**: Out of compulsion. We give in this manner when we feel like someone is trying to take what is ours. We may give because we feel obligated. Some have this attitude because they believe they own the resources. They want to hold on to the resources because they see them as their own. Either we manage our stuff, or we invest God's possessions. We shouldn't be made to give; we should want to do so.
- **The Right Way**: Cheerfully. We give in this manner when we have a passion for God and see resources as belonging to Him. We see ourselves as stockbrokers. Our stock is in God, and we become financial planners for the purpose of others taking stock in Him.

Q: Do you ever feel pressure to use your money in a certain way? If so, how does it make your feel?

Knowing God's definition of generosity

"And God is able to make all grace abound to you, so that in all things at all times, having all that you need, you will abound in every good work" (2 Corinthians 9:8). God wants us to be generous in our giving. A simple definition is giving what we have to meet the needs of others who don't have. The word *generous* has to do with what we give. Those who are able to give generously can do so because God has given to them generously. God has given to us to meet our needs and has provided enough for us to be generous in order to meet the needs around us.

Q: Do you believe God gives generously? Why or why not?

Knowing why God gives generously

"And God is able to make all grace abound to you, so that in all things at all times, having all that you need, you will abound in every good work" (2 Corinthians 9:8). He gives generously because He loves us and He wants us to use what He gives to show His love to others. God gives generously to me so that I can give generously to those around me. Read the verse from above again. I need to remember the "Abounding Principle," which says: "I do good work when God gives me

the fully devoted life

the fuel to do good work." Grace is the fuel. Paul taught us that grace abounds to us, that grace comes to us in sufficient amounts for us to have enough to give to others. He wrote that we are to abound in every good work. Grace is giving people what they don't deserve. When we want to give grace, we find ways to show grace. One way to do so is by giving resources to meet the needs of others. If there is no grace, often there is no giving. The grace we receive from God, a love that we don't deserve, causes us to be more compassionate toward people who also need to receive God's love. The love we receive provides the energy and motivation to invest.

Q: How much do you love the people around you? One way we can answer this question is to see how much we give to meet their needs. What does your spending say about your love for people?

Knowing God's definition of being rich

"Now he who supplies seed to the sower and bread for food will also supply and increase your store of seed and will enlarge the harvest of your righteousness. You will be made rich in every way so that you can be generous on every occasion, and through us your generosity will result in thanksgiving to God" (2 Corinthians 9:10-11). How would you define being rich? Do you consider yourself a have or a have not? Economically, we often refer to people as either haves or have nots.

People have different ideas about who the rich are and what God expects of us in relationship to money. God helps us see who the rich are through His Word. This teaching is closely related to what we learned about generosity. When are we rich? We're rich when we have enough to meet our needs and to help meet the needs of others. That definition is God's.

Paul taught that God increases our store of seed. He does so to bring a wealth that is shared. This truth is awesome. God's criterion for being rich is to have enough to share. God is not concerned with the amount that we have to share but with the fact that we have enough to share. Paul taught that we're rich in every way so that we can be generous in every occasion. The word *rich* is connected with what we have, and the word *generous* is connected with what we give. Some are rich, but they just aren't generous! God wants us to have enough to be able to invest generously as needs arise. In other words, God wants us to be rich!

Q: How does the world define the rich?

Q: How does the world define the poor?

Q: Do you meet God's criteria of being rich?

Q: What needs have you noticed that you could help through giving your money?

Creating room in my budget so that I can give

We get excited easily when we know that our gift is making a difference. We should give because God instructs us to do so; however, we want to be obedient when we know we are impacting the world for Him. When the desire to invest in others becomes great enough, we manage our finances to ensure there is margin so we can give.

The word *margin* is an important word to consider. To have margin is to have something that is uncommitted and usable. For example, you may have a margin of time. You have time during the day that is uncommitted that you could use to invest in meaningful ways. The same is true of finances. To have financial margin is to have monies that are uncommitted that can be used to invest in God's kingdom.

Many aren't obedient in giving because they have no margin. Overextending ourselves and finding ourselves without the financial resources to meet our commitments is easy. Instead of having margin, we overspend, and our overspending brings stress.

What do we do if we have no margin? When we have no margin, we naturally take out expenses that we consider unnecessary. Unfortunately, many times, we consider giving to God unnecessary. One of the problems with this perspective is the way we think about our giving to God, which is a heart thing. Those who go from seeing their giving to God as an investment to seeing that giving as an expense lose sight of the importance of the use of their finances. The truth is that the best way to approach our budget is to have one that prioritizes investments first. When we do so, we manage our budgets in order to make the investment. Everything depends on where our giving to investments lies on the financial priority chain. As you prepare for the income you will earn in the future, it's important that you consider where you invest funds and the impact it will have. The great thing about giving to God is that the investment has eternal dividends.

God, I want to be obedient to You in my giving. I ask You to help me as I manage Your resources in a way that leads me toward fully obeying You. Please keep my eyes on those who will be impacted because of the investments I make for You.

Section Six
Totally:
A Life to Surrender

Chapter Ten
The Commitments:
Imagine a life that dedicates all to God.

> One of the teachers of the law came and heard them debating. Noticing that Jesus had given them a good answer, he asked him, "Of all the commandments, which is the most important?" "The most important one," answered Jesus, "is this: 'Hear, O Israel, the Lord our God, the Lord is one. Love the Lord your God with all your heart and with all your soul and with all your mind and with all your strength.' The second is this: 'Love your neighbor as yourself.' There is no commandment greater than these."
>
> Mark 12:28-31

We've been on an amazing journey through this study. Remember how we began? We started with taking a look at who we are in regards to sharing our testimony, spending our time, using our talents, and giving our treasures. We accomplished this examination by completing the spiritual assessment. Go back to chapter one where the assessment is located and look again at the Spider Graph which includes your responses. Are you pleased with the graph? If you took it over right now, what would it look like? Let's do it! Complete the Spiritual Assessment Test below once again.

Instructions: Using the scale from one to ten, with one meaning never true and ten meaning always true, answer the following questions.

TESTIMONY

Sharing my story with those who don't know God

1. I have a burden for those who do not know Christ.

   "When he saw the crowds, he had compassion on them, because they were harassed and helpless, like sheep without a shepherd" (Matthew 9:36).

   Score: _____

2. I identify those in my circle of influence who are lost.

   "For the Son of Man came to seek and to save what was lost" (Luke 19:10).

   Score: _____

3. I pray regularly for those in my circle of influence who are lost.

   "My prayer is not for them alone. I pray also for those who will believe in me through their message" (John 17:20).

   Score: _____

4. I share my faith with others regularly.

   "For we cannot help speaking about what we have seen and heard" (Acts 4:20).

   Score: _____

5. I use my spiritual gifts to serve others in an effort to build relationships with the lost.

   "It was he who gave some to be apostles, some to be prophets, some to be evangelists, and some to be pastors and teachers, to prepare God's people for works of service" (Ephesians 4:11-12).

   Score: _____

6. I invite those in my circle of influence to experiences where they will be exposed to the message of Christ.

"Go to the street corners and invite to the banquet anyone you find" (Matthew 22:9).

Score: _____

7. allow God to use me as a witness by living a life free of sin.

"Finally, brothers, whatever is true, whatever is noble, whatever is right, whatever is pure, whatever is lovely, whatever is admirable—if anything is excellent or praiseworthy—think about such things" (Philippians 4:8).
Score: _____

8. My words and my actions support one another.

"'About Jesus of Nazareth,' they replied. 'He was a prophet, powerful in word and deed before God and all the people'" (Luke 24:19).

Score: _____

9. I live a life of joy.

"But the fruit of the Spirit is...joy" (Galatians 5:22).

Score: _____

10. I am willing to put myself at risk in an effort to share the good news of Christ with those who are lost.

"For even the Son of Man did not come to be served, but to serve, and to give his life as a ransom for many" (Mark 10:45).

Score: _____

TIME

Growing in my relationship with God

1. I have a close companionship with God.

   "A man of many companions may come to ruin, but there is a friend who sticks closer than a brother" (Proverbs 18:24).

   Score: _____

2. I spend time alone with God on a regular basis.

   "In the morning, O LORD, you hear my voice; in the morning I lay my requests before you and wait in expectation" (Psalm 5:3).

   Score: _____

3. I regularly practice the discipline of prayer.

   "And pray in the Spirit on all occasions with all kinds of prayers and requests. With this in mind, be alert and always keep on praying for all the saints" (Ephesians 6:18).

   Score: _____

4. I regularly practice the discipline of Bible study.

   "Your word is a lamp to my feet and a light for my path" (Psalm 119:105).

   Score: _____

5. I regularly memorize God's Word.

   "I have hidden your word in my heart that I might not sin against you" (Psalm 119:11).

   Score: _____

6. I live a life of self control.

"But the fruit of the Spirit is…self control" (Galatians 5:22-23).

Score: _____

7. I regularly spend time with a group of believers who hold me accountable to living obediently.

"Every day they continued to meet together in the temple courts. They broke bread in their homes and ate together with glad and sincere hearts" (Acts 2:46).

Score: _____

8. I worship God corporately weekly.

"You Samaritans worship what you do not know; we worship what we do know, for salvation is from the Jews" (John 4:22).

Score: _____

9. I am regularly mentored by another believer.

"Don't let anyone look down on you because you are young, but set an example for the believers in speech, in life, in love, in faith and in purity" (1Timothy 4:12).

Score: _____

10. I work with God to overcome my weaknesses.

"If you are pleased with me, teach me your ways so I may know you and continue to find favor with you" (Exodus 33:13).

Score: _____

TALENTS

Using my gifts and talents in service

1. I regularly put the needs of others before my own needs.
"The Son of Man did not come to be served, but to serve, and to give his life as a ransom for many" (Matthew 20:28).
Score: _____

2. I am concerned about those who are in need.
"But a Samaritan, as he traveled, came where the man was; and when he saw him, he took pity on him" (Luke 10:33).
Score: _____

3. I pray for those who are in need.
"We always thank God, the Father of our Lord Jesus Christ, when we pray for you" (Colossians 1:3).
Score: _____

4. I actively seek ways to help those who are in need.
"For I was hungry and you gave me something to eat, I was thirsty and you gave me something to drink, I was a stranger and you invited me in, I needed clothes and you clothed me, I was sick and you looked after me, I was in prison and you came to visit me" (Matthew 25:35-36).
Score: _____

5. I am kind to strangers.
"I was a stranger and you invited me in" (Matthew 25:35).
Score: _____

6. I know what my spiritual gifts are.

"Therefore you do not lack any spiritual gift as you eagerly wait for our Lord Jesus Christ to be revealed" (1 Corinthians 1:7).

Score: _____

7. I have an active ministry.

"The King will reply, 'I tell you the truth, whatever you did for one of the least of these brothers of mine, you did for me'" (Matthew 25:40).

Score: _____

8. I serve others even when it is not convenient.

"You, my brothers, were called to be free. But do not use your freedom to indulge the sinful nature; rather, serve one another in love" (Galatians 5:13).

Score: _____

9. I pray for those who are in leadership within the church.

"Pray for us. We are sure that we have a clear conscience and desire to live honorably in every way" (Hebrews 13:18).

Score: _____

10. I make time sacrifices to meet the needs of others.

"Be imitators of God, therefore, as dearly loved children and live a life of love, just as Christ loved us and gave himself up for us as a fragrant offering and sacrifice to God" (Ephesians 5:1-2).

Score: _____

TREASURES
Managing resources to make a difference

1. I give my tithe to assist in God's kingdom work.

"*'Bring the whole tithe into the storehouse, that there may be food in my house. Test me in this,' says the LORD Almighty, 'and see if I will not throw open the floodgates of heaven and pour out so much blessing that you will not have room enough for it'*" (Malachi 3:10).

Score: _____

2. I trust God in every situation.

"*Do not let your hearts be troubled. Trust in God; trust also in me*" (John 14:1).

Score: _____

3. I regularly make sacrifices to please God.

"*Greater love has no one than this, that he lay down his life for his friends*" (John 15:13).

Score: _____

4. I give cheerfully to advance God's kingdom.

"*Each man should give what he has decided in his heart to give, not reluctantly or under compulsion, for God loves a cheerful giver*" (2 Corinthians 9:7).

Score: _____

5. I have a desire to be obedient in giving (to give what is in my heart).

"*But just as you excel in everything—in faith, in speech, in knowledge, in complete earnestness and in your love for us— see that you also excel in this grace of giving*" (2 Corinthians 8:7).

Score: _____

6. My actions reveal that I believe money and resources are God's possessions which are under my care.
"All the believers were one in heart and mind. No one claimed that any of his possessions was his own, but they shared everything they had" (Acts 4:32).
Score: _____

7. I consider how my purchases affect my ability to give to God's kingdom before I make them.
"Then he said to them, 'Watch out! Be on your guard against all kinds of greed; a man's life does not consist in the abundance of his possessions'" (Luke 12:15).
Score: _____

8. I ask, "Will this purchase honor God?" before spending money.
"Jesus answered, 'If you want to be perfect, go, sell your possessions and give to the poor, and you will have treasure in heaven. Then come, follow me'" (Matthew 19:21).
Score: _____

9. I manage my resources to ensure margin (available funds) to help those in need.
"But Zacchaeus stood up and said to the Lord, 'Look, Lord! Here and now I give half of my possessions to the poor, and if I have cheated anybody out of anything, I will pay back four times the amount'" (Luke 19:8).
Score: _____

10. I am willing to sacrifice to invest in the success of others.
"Selling their possessions and goods, they gave to anyone as he had need" (Acts 2:45).
Score: _____

On the next page, plot your score!

Plotting My Score

It's time to plot our scores again. If you need to look over the instructions, go back to Chapter One. Start plotting!

The Spider Graph

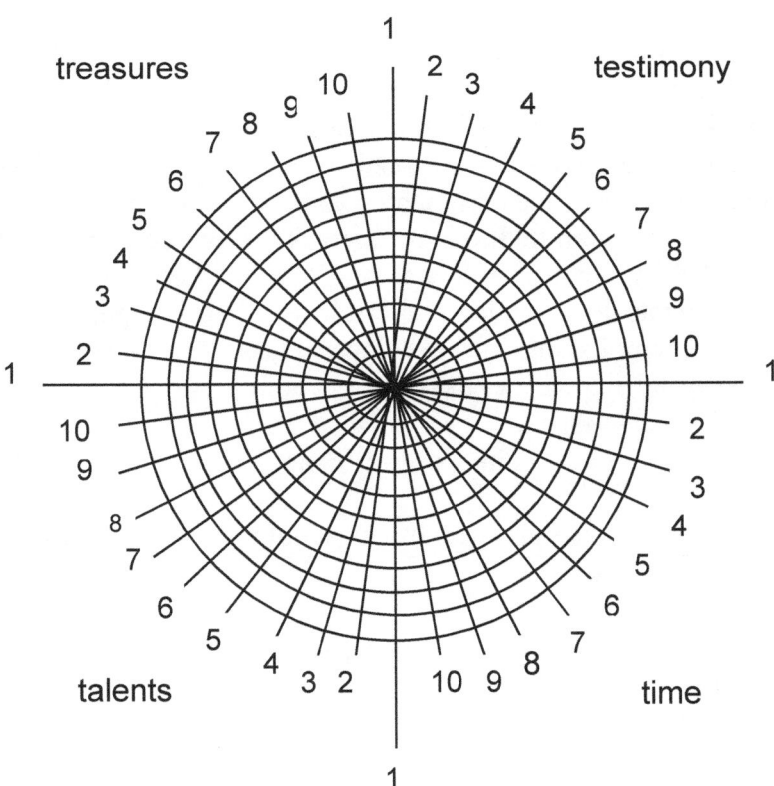

Q: Does the new Spider Graph look any different than the old one? Why did this change occur?

No one expects you to have mastered all of the elements of maturing in the Christian life over these few weeks. The good news is that you now have the resources to use as you continue and know what areas need your attention. You may need to take special classes or more directed studies in areas of weakness. You may need to purchase a book that focuses on areas of needed growth. You may need to get into a small group or find someone who can help you one on one as you grow. If so, search out those opportunities. Keep taking the Spiritual Assessment Test as you continue to mature in your faith. You may want to take it every three or four months to see if you're improving. Doing so will help you keep the areas that need attention in the spotlight. A Spider Graph is included in the back of the book (Appendix B) for you to copy. Feel free to make as many copies as you want.

Are you committed to stay on track? Are you committed to be a fully devoted follower of Christ? Below are some commitments to consider prayerfully. If you're passionate about accomplishing these things, check the appropriate response and sign it. Let the journey continue!

The Commitments

- ➢ I commit to be open with others about my faith in Christ.
  __Yes __No

- ➢ I commit to dedicate appropriate time for my spiritual growth.
  __Yes __No
- ➢ I commit to use my gifts and talents in acts of service to impact the world.
  __Yes __No

- ➢ I commit to be faithful in managing the resources under my care to be obedient in giving what God desires.
  __Yes __No

- I commit to being a "partial giver" who's moving toward full obedience.
  __Yes __No

- I commit to being a "whole giver," obediently giving my tithe.
  __Yes __No

- I commit to being an "over giver," giving to the passions of my heart.
  __Yes __No

_____
Signature

_____
Date

God, I ask You to help me as I do what's necessary to know You more, serve You more, and share You more. I thank You for loving me and wanting the best for me. You are my God, and I long to honor You!

End Notes

Chapter Two
1. Tim Keller, *The Reason for God* (New York: Dutton, 2008), 275-276.

Chapter Four
3. Max Lucado, *The Applause of Heaven* (Nashville, TN: Word, 1990), 114-116.
4. Chuck Colson, "Bottoms Up: Is Change Possible?" *Breakpoint Newsletter*, December 15, 2006, 1.

Chapter Five
5. Mark Buchanan, "Singing in the Chains," *Christianity Today,* February 2008, 33.
6. Tom Brady, "Tom Brady on the Future," transcript of *60 Minutes*, cbsnews.com, December 23, 2007, http://www.cbsnews.com/sections/i_video/main500251.shtml?id=3643660n?source=search_video.
7. Associated Press, "Study: Babies can tell helpful, hurtful playmates," CNN.com, November 21, 2007, http://www.cnn.com/2007/HEALTH/11/21/infant.judging.ap/index.html.
8. Thomas L. Friedman, "The Whole World is Watching," *New York Times*, June 27, 2007.
9. Gary Thomas, *The Beautiful Fight* (Grand Rapids, MI: Zondervan, 2007), 63.

Chapter Six
10. Anne Cetas, "Serving Together," *Our Daily Bread,* June 2008, 7.

Chapter Seven
11. Shirley Shaw, "Look at the Children!" *Today's Christian,* September/October 2007, 46.
12. Reggie McNeal, *The Present Future* (San Francisco, CA: Jossey-Bass, 2003), 98.

13. Frederick Buechner, *Wishful Thinking: A Seeker's ABC* (New York, NY: HarperOne, 1993), 119.
14. Bruce Bugbee, Don Cousins, and Bill Hybels, *Network: The Right People...In the Right Places...For the Right Reasons* (Grand Rapids, MI: Zondervan, 1994), 47-55.

Chapter Eight
15. Craig L. Blomberg, *Preaching the Parables* (Grand Rapids, MI: Baker Academic, 2004), 51.
16. Felix Dennis, "Giving Away a Fortune," *The Week*, September 15, 2006, 15.
17. Kevin G. Harney, *Seismic Shifts* (Grand Rapids, MI: Zondervan, 2005), 200.
18. Dan Ewald, "It's not About Me," *Christian Reader*, January/February 2004, 18.
19. Clarence Hackett, *Christian Financial Planning* (Jacksonville: Florida Baptist Convention, 2000), 11-18.

Appendix A

The QT Guides

Week One
Day One

Topic: A burden for those who do not know Christ.

Scripture: Matthew 9:36; Matthew 14:14; Colossians 3:8-14

- **Summarize:** Summarize the Scripture in your own words.

- **Reflection:** What is God trying to teach you through this passage?

- **Key Verse:** What is the key verse that stands out to you as most important? Write it in the space provided.

- **Action:** What does God want you to do about what you have learned?

Week One
Day Two

Topic: Identifying those in my circle of influence who are lost.

Scripture: Luke 19:1-10

- **Summarize**: Summarize the Scripture in your own words.

- **Reflection**: What is God trying to teach you through this passage?

- **Key Verse**: What is the key verse that stands out to you as most important? Write it in the space provided.

- **Action**: What does God want you to do about what you have learned?

Week One
Day Three

Topic: Praying daily for those in my circle of influence who are lost.

Scripture: John 17:1-26

- **Summarize**: Summarize the Scripture in your own words.

- **Reflection**: What is God trying to teach you through this passage?

- **Key Verse**: What is the key verse that stands out to you as most important? Write it in the space provided.

- **Action**: What does God want you to do about what you have learned?

Week One
Day Four

Topic: Sharing my faith with others daily.

Scripture: Acts 4:1-20

- **Summarize:** Summarize the Scripture in your own words.

- **Reflection:** What is God trying to teach you through this passage?

- **Key Verse:** What is the key verse that stands out to you as most important? Write it in the space provided.

- **Action:** What does God want you to do about what you have learned?

Week One
Day Five

Topic: Using my spiritual gifts to serve others in an effort to build relationships with the lost.

Scripture: 1 Corinthians 12:4-6, 12-31

- **Summarize**: Summarize the Scripture in your own words.

- **Reflection**: What is God trying to teach you through this passage?

- **Key Verse**: What is the key verse that stands out to you as most important? Write it in the space provided.

- **Action**: What does God want you to do about what you have learned?

Week Two
Day One

Topic: Inviting those in my circle of influence to come to events where they will be exposed to the message of Christ.

Scripture: Matthew 22:1-14

- **Summarize:** Summarize the Scripture in your own words.

- **Reflection:** What is God trying to teach you through this passage?

- **Key Verse:** What is the key verse that stands out to you as most important? Write it in the space provided.

- **Action:** What does God want you to do about what you have learned?

Week Two
Day Two

Topic: Allowing God to use me as a witness by living a life free of sin.

Scripture: Philippians 3:12-21; Philippians 4:8-9

- **Summarize:** Summarize the Scripture in your own words.

- **Reflection:** What is God trying to teach you through this passage?

- **Key Verse:** What is the key verse that stands out to you as most important? Write it in the space provided.

- **Action:** What does God want you to do about what you have learned?

Week Two
Day Three

Topic: Using my words and my actions to support one another.

Scripture: Luke 24:19; James 1:22-27

- **Summarize:** Summarize the Scripture in your own words.

- **Reflection:** What is God trying to teach you through this passage?

- **Key Verse:** What is the key verse that stands out to you as most important? Write it in the space provided.

- **Action:** What does God want you to do about what you have learned?

Week Two
Day Four

Topic: Living a life of joy.

Scripture: Galatians 5:13-6:10

- **Summarize**: Summarize the Scripture in your own words.

- **Reflection**: What is God trying to teach you through this passage?

- **Key Verse**: What is the key verse that stands out to you as most important? Write it in the space provided.

- **Action**: What does God want you to do about what you have learned?

Week Two
Day Five

Topic: Being willing to put myself at risk in an effort to share the Good News of Christ with those who are lost.

Scripture: Mark 10:45; Matthew 10:16-42

- **Summarize:** Summarize the Scripture in your own words.

- **Reflection:** What is God trying to teach you through this passage?

- **Key Verse:** What is the key verse that stands out to you as most important? Write it in the space provided.

- **Action:** What does God want you to do about what you have learned?

Week Three
Day One

Topic: Having a close companionship with God.

Scripture: Proverbs 15:1-17; Proverbs 18:24

- **Summarize**: Summarize the Scripture in your own words.

- **Reflection**: What is God trying to teach you through this passage?

- **Key Verse**: What is the key verse that stands out to you as most important? Write it in the space provided.

- **Action**: What does God want you to do about what you have learned?

Week Three
Day Two

Topic: Spending time alone with God on a daily basis.

Scripture: Psalm 5:3; Luke 5:15-16; Luke 6:12-13; Luke 11:1-4

- **Summarize:** Summarize the Scripture in your own words.

- **Reflection:** What is God trying to teach you through this passage?

- **Key Verse:** What is the key verse that stands out to you as most important? Write it in the space provided.

- **Action:** What does God want you to do about what you have learned?

Week Three
Day Three

Topic: Daily practicing the discipline of prayer.

Scripture: Ephesians 6:18; James 5:13-18

- **Summarize:** Summarize the Scripture in your own words.

- **Reflection:** What is God trying to teach you through this passage?

- **Key Verse:** What is the key verse that stands out to you as most important? Write it in the space provided.

- **Action:** What does God want you to do about what you have learned?

Week Three
Day Four

Topic: Daily practicing the discipline of Bible study.

Scripture: Psalm 119:105; 2 Timothy 3:14 – 4:5

- **Summarize:** Summarize the Scripture in your own words.

- **Reflection:** What is God trying to teach you through this passage?

- **Key Verse:** What is the key verse that stands out to you as most important? Write it in the space provided.

- **Action:** What does God want you to do about what you have learned?

Week Three
Day Five

Topic: Regularly memorizing God's Word.

Scripture: Psalm 119:1-40

- **Summarize:** Summarize the Scripture in your own words.

- **Reflection:** What is God trying to teach you through this passage?

- **Key Verse:** What is the key verse that stands out to you as most important? Write it in the space provided.

- **Action:** What does God want you to do about what you have learned?

Week Four
Day One

Topic: Living a life of self-control.

Scripture: Galatians 5:22-23; Romans 8:5-14

- **Summarize:** Summarize the Scripture in your own words.

- **Reflection:** What is God trying to teach you through this passage?

- **Key Verse:** What is the key verse that stands out to you as most important? Write it in the space provided.

- **Action:** What does God want you to do about what you have learned?

Week Four
Day Two

Topic: Attending a group meeting with believers who hold me accountable to living obediently.

Scripture: Acts 2:46; Hebrews 10:23-25; Proverbs 27:6; Proverbs 27:17

- **Summarize**: Summarize the Scripture in your own words.

- **Reflection**: What is God trying to teach you through this passage?

- **Key Verse**: What is the key verse that stands out to you as most important? Write it in the space provided.

- **Action**: What does God want you to do about what you have learned?

Week Four
Day Three

Topic: Worshiping God corporately weekly.

Scripture: John 4:5-30, 39-42

- **Summarize:** Summarize the Scripture in your own words.

- **Reflection:** What is God trying to teach you through this passage?

- **Key Verse:** What is the key verse that stands out to you as most important? Write it in the space provided.

- **Action:** What does God want you to do about what you have learned?

Week Four
Day Four

Topic: Regularly being mentored by another believer.

Scripture: 1 Timothy 4:12; Philemon 1:1-7; Titus 2:1-7

- **Summarize**: Summarize the Scripture in your own words.

- **Reflection**: What is God trying to teach you through this passage?

- **Key Verse**: What is the key verse that stands out to you as most important? Write it in the space provided.

- **Action**: What does God want you to do about what you have learned?

Week Four
Day Five

Topic: Working with God to overcome my weaknesses.

Scripture: Exodus 33:13; Romans 7:14 – 8:4

- **Summarize:** Summarize the Scripture in your own words.

- **Reflection:** What is God trying to teach you through this passage?

- **Key Verse:** What is the key verse that stands out to you as most important? Write it in the space provided.

- **Action:** What does God want you to do about what you have learned?

Week Five
Day One

Topic: Regularly putting the needs of others before my own needs.

Scripture: Matthew 20:26-28; Philippians 1:27-2:11

- **Summarize**: Summarize the Scripture in your own words.

- **Reflection**: What is God trying to teach you through this passage?

- **Key Verse**: What is the key verse that stands out to you as most important? Write it in the space provided.

- **Action**: What does God want you to do about what you have learned?

Week Five
Day Two

Topic: Being concerned about those who are in need.

Scripture: Luke 10:25-37

- **Summarize:** Summarize the Scripture in your own words.

- **Reflection:** What is God trying to teach you through this passage?

- **Key Verse:** What is the key verse that stands out to you as most important? Write it in the space provided.

- **Action:** What does God want you to do about what you have learned?

Week Five
Day Three

Topic: Praying for those who are in need.

Scripture: Colossians 1:3; Deuteronomy 15:4-11

- **Summarize:** Summarize the Scripture in your own words.

- **Reflection:** What is God trying to teach you through this passage?

- **Key Verse:** What is the key verse that stands out to you as most important? Write it in the space provided.

- **Action:** What does God want you to do about what you have learned?

Week Five
Day Four

Topic: Actively seeking ways to help those who are in need.

Scripture: Matthew 25:31-46

- **Summarize:** Summarize the Scripture in your own words.

- **Reflection:** What is God trying to teach you through this passage?

- **Key Verse:** What is the key verse that stands out to you as most important? Write it in the space provided.

- **Action:** What does God want you to do about what you have learned?

Week Five
Day Five

Topic: Being kind to strangers.

Scripture: Matthew 25:35; Colossians 4:2-6; 2 Peter 1:3-9

- **Summarize**: Summarize the Scripture in your own words.

- **Reflection**: What is God trying to teach you through this passage?

- **Key Verse**: What is the key verse that stands out to you as most important? Write it in the space provided.

- **Action**: What does God want you to do about what you have learned?

Week Six
Day One

Topic: Discovering my spiritual gifts.

Scripture: 1 Corinthians 1:7; Romans 12:1-21

- **Summarize:** Summarize the Scripture in your own words.

- **Reflection:** What is God trying to teach you through this passage?

- **Key Verse:** What is the key verse that stands out to you as most important? Write it in the space provided.

- **Action:** What does God want you to do about what you have learned?

Week Six
Day Two

Topic: Having an active ministry

Scripture: Matthew 25:40; Ephesians 4:1-13

- **Summarize:** Summarize the Scripture in your own words.

- **Reflection:** What is God trying to teach you through this passage?

- **Key Verse:** What is the key verse that stands out to you as most important? Write it in the space provided.

- **Action:** What does God want you to do about what you have learned?

Week Six
Day Three

Topic: Serving others when it is not convenient.

Scripture: Galatians 5:13; Hebrews 6:10-12; 2 Timothy 4:5-8

- **Summarize:** Summarize the Scripture in your own words.

- **Reflection:** What is God trying to teach you through this passage?

- **Key Verse:** What is the key verse that stands out to you as most important? Write it in the space provided.

- **Action:** What does God want you to do about what you have learned?

Week Six
Day Four

Topic: Praying for those who are in leadership within the church.

Scripture: Hebrews 13:17-21

- **Summarize:** Summarize the Scripture in your own words.

- **Reflection:** What is God trying to teach you through this passage?

- **Key Verse:** What is the key verse that stands out to you as most important? Write it in the space provided.

- **Action:** What does God want you to do about what you have learned?

Week Six
Day Five

Topic: Making time sacrifices to meet the needs of others.

Scripture: Ephesians 4:32-5:2; Matthew 9:35-38

- **Summarize:** Summarize the Scripture in your own words.

- **Reflection:** What is God trying to teach you through this passage?

- **Key Verse:** What is the key verse that stands out to you as most important? Write it in the space provided.

- **Action:** What does God want you to do about what you have learned?

**Week Seven
Day One**

Topic: Giving my tithe to assist in God's kingdom work.

Scripture: Malachi 3:10; 1 Corinthians 16:1-3; Leviticus 27:30

- **Summarize**: Summarize the Scripture in your own words.

- **Reflection**: What is God trying to teach you through this passage?

- **Key Verse**: What is the key verse that stands out to you as most important? Write it in the space provided.

- **Action**: What does God want you to do about what you have learned?

Week Seven
Day Two

Topic: Trusting God in every situation.

Scripture: John 14:1; Luke 12:22-34

- **Summarize:** Summarize the Scripture in your own words.

- **Reflection:** What is God trying to teach you through this passage?

- **Key Verse:** What is the key verse that stands out to you as most important? Write it in the space provided.

- **Action:** What does God want you to do about what you have learned?

Week Seven
Day Three

Topic: Regularly making sacrifices to please God.

Scripture: John 15:13; 2 Corinthians 8:1-15

- **Summarize:** Summarize the Scripture in your own words.

- **Reflection:** What is God trying to teach you through this passage?

- **Key Verse:** What is the key verse that stands out to you as most important? Write it in the space provided.

- **Action:** What does God want you to do about what you have learned?

Week Seven
Day Four

Topic: Giving cheerfully to advance God's kingdom.

Scripture: 2 Corinthians 9:6-15

- **Summarize:** Summarize the Scripture in your own words.

- **Reflection:** What is God trying to teach you through this passage?

- **Key Verse:** What is the key verse that stands out to you as most important? Write it in the space provided.

- **Action:** What does God want you to do about what you have learned?

**Week Seven
Day Five**

Topic: Having a desire to be obedient in giving.

Scripture: 2 Corinthians 8:7; Mark 12:41-44

- **Summarize**: Summarize the Scripture in your own words.

- **Reflection**: What is God trying to teach you through this passage?

- **Key Verse**: What is the key verse that stands out to you as most important? Write it in the space provided.

- **Action**: What does God want you to do about what you have learned?

Week Eight
Day One

Topic: Considering money and resources to be God's possessions which are under my care.

Scripture: Proverbs 15:6; Acts 4:32; Matthew 25:14-30

- **Summarize:** Summarize the Scripture in your own words.

- **Reflection:** What is God trying to teach you through this passage?

- **Key Verse:** What is the key verse that stands out to you as most important? Write it in the space provided.

- **Action:** What does God want you to do about what you have learned?

Week Eight
Day Two

Topic: Considering how my purchases affect my ability to give to God's kingdom before I make them.

Scripture: Luke 12:15; Hebrews 13:5-7

- **Summarize:** Summarize the Scripture in your own words.

- **Reflection:** What is God trying to teach you through this passage?

- **Key Verse:** What is the key verse that stands out to you as most important? Write it in the space provided.

- **Action:** What does God want you to do about what you have learned?

Week Eight
Day Three

Topic: Asking "Will this purchase honor God?" before spending money.

Scripture: Matthew 19:21; 1 Corinthians 10:31-11:1; James 5:1-6

- **Summarize**: Summarize the Scripture in your own words.

- **Reflection**: What is God trying to teach you through this passage?

- **Key Verse**: What is the key verse that stands out to you as most important? Write it in the space provided.

- **Action**: What does God want you to do about what you have learned?

Week Eight
Day Four

Topic: Managing money and resources to ensure there is margin (available funds) to help those in need.

Scripture: Luke 19:8; Luke 14:27-35

- **Summarize:** Summarize the Scripture in your own words.

- **Reflection:** What is God trying to teach you through this passage?

- **Key Verse:** What is the key verse that stands out to you as most important? Write it in the space provided.

- **Action:** What does God want you to do about what you have learned?

Week Eight
Day Five

Topic: Being willing to sacrifice to invest in the success of others.

Scripture: Acts 2:45; Luke 18:18-30

- **Summarize:** Summarize the Scripture in your own words.

- **Reflection:** What is God trying to teach you through this passage?

- **Key Verse:** What is the key verse that stands out to you as most important? Write it in the space provided.

- **Action:** What does God want you to do about what you have learned?

225

Appendix B

The Spider Graph

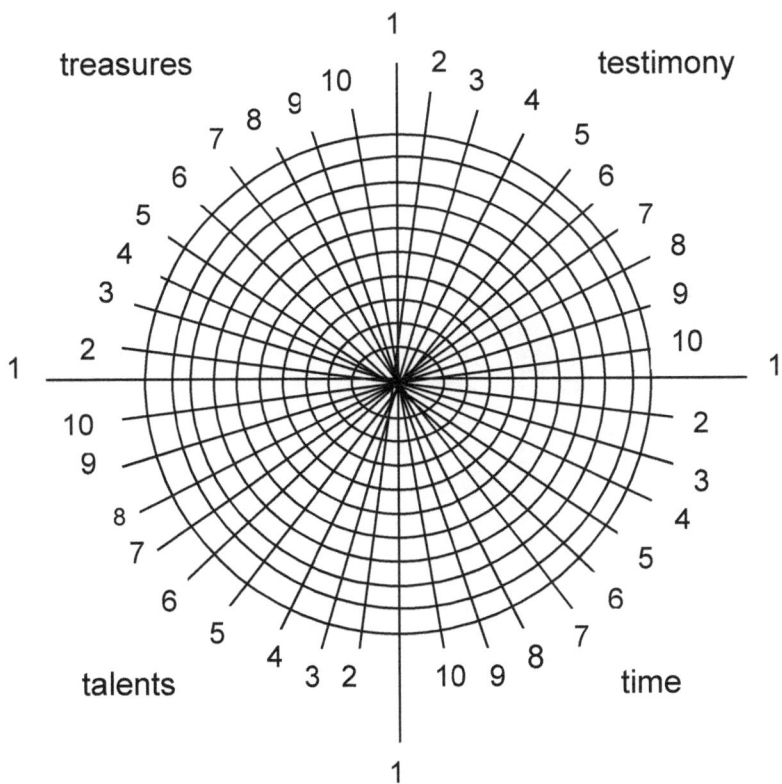

www.ingramcontent.com/pod-product-compliance
Lightning Source LLC
Chambersburg PA
CBHW032109090426
42743CB00007B/295